CW00750984

THE 36 SECRET STRATEGIES OF THE MARTIAL ARTS

OF THE

MARTIAL ARTS

The Classic Chinese Guide for Success in War, Business, and Life

Hiroshi Moriya

FOREWORD AND TRANSLATION BY
William Scott Wilson

KODANSHA INTERNATIONAL
Tokyo · New York · London

Calligraphy by Ui Kenho

Based on the revised edition of *Heiho sanjuroku kei* by Hiroshi Moriya published in Japanese by Mikasa Shobo in 2004.

Distributed in the United States by Kodansha America, Inc., and in the United Kingdom and continental Europe by Kodansha Europe Ltd.

Published by Kodansha International Ltd., 17–14 Otowa 1-chome, Bunkyo-ku, Tokyo 112–8652, and Kodansha America, Inc.

First edition, 2008
15 14 13 12 11 10 09 08   10 9 8 7 6 5 4 3 2 1

Library of Congress Catalogue-in-Publication Data available

www.kodansha-intl.com

CONTENTS

FOREWORD William Scott Wilson   7

INTRODUCTION   11

OPENING REMARKS: ANCHOR ON REALITY   15

PART I **STRATEGIES FOR VICTORY IN BATTLE**   19

Strategy 1   Obscure Heaven, Cross the Sea   21

Strategy 2   Surround Wei, Help Chao   27

Strategy 3   Borrow a Sword to Make Your Kill   33

Strategy 4   Await His Tired Steps at Your Leisure   39

Strategy 5   Take Advantage of the Fire to Plunder the Goods   47

Strategy 6   Be Heard in the East, Attack from the West   53

PART II **STRATEGIES FOR ENGAGING THE ENEMY**   59

Strategy 7   Create Existence from Nonexistence   61

Strategy 8   Cross Over to Ch'en Ts'ang in the Dark   67

Strategy 9   On the Distant Shore, Watch for Fire   73

Strategy 10   Conceal a Sword behind a Smile   79

Strategy 11   Sacrifice the Peach to Secure the Plum   85

Strategy 12   Lead Away the Sheep When Conditions Are Right   91

PART III **STRATEGIES FOR ATTACK**   95

Strategy 13   Beat the Grass, Surprise the Snake   97

Strategy 14   Borrow the Corpse, Revive Its Soul   101

Strategy 15   Pacify the Tiger Then Lead It from the Mountain   107

Strategy 16   If You Covet It, Leave It Alone   113

Strategy 17   Cast a Brick, Pull in Jade   119

Strategy 18   To Catch a Thief, Catch His King   125

PART **IV   STRATEGIES FOR
          AMBIGUOUS SITUATIONS**   131

Strategy 19   Pull the Firewood from under the Kettle   133

Strategy 20   Disturb the Water, Grab the Fish   139

Strategy 21   The Golden Cicada Sheds Its Shell   145

Strategy 22   Bar the Door, Grab the Thief   151

Strategy 23   Befriend Those at a Distance, Attack Those Nearby   157

Strategy 24   Borrow a Road, Attack Kuo   161

PART **V   STRATEGIES FOR UNIFIED BATTLE**   167

Strategy 25   Steal the Beams, Replace the Pillars   169

Strategy 26   Point to the Mulberry, Berate the Pagoda Tree   173

Strategy 27   Feign Stupidity, Do Not Be Injudicious   179

Strategy 28   Send Them to the Roof, Remove the Ladder   185

Strategy 29   Make the Flowers Bloom on the Tree   193

Strategy 30   Quit as Guest, Take Over as Host   199

PART **VI   STRATEGIES FOR A LOST BATTLE**   205

Strategy 31   The Strategy of the Beautiful Woman   207

Strategy 32   The Strategy of the Empty Fortress   213

Strategy 33   Create a Rift   219

Strategy 34   The Strategy of Self-Injury   225

Strategy 35   The Strategy of Links   231

Strategy 36   Retreat Is Considered the Best   237

NOTES   243

BIBLIOGRAPHY   255

FOREWORD

Legend has it that when Yamamoto Kansuke[1] was to be retained by the young warlord Takeda Shingen,[2] one of Shingen's most important vassals, in the presence of the warlord and his retainers, suddenly challenged him to a duel. Kansuke, a strong swordsman of the Kyoto style, had only one eye, was lame, and was missing a few of his fingers. He was also a ronin not originally from Shingen's fief, and his loyalty, in the eyes of the challenger, was dubious.

This challenge was unexpected, but Kansuke readily accepted it, insisting, however, that it be called a "battle" rather than a duel. Kansuke further insisted that, in light of his physical disabilities, this battle should be fought in a small boat that was anchored offshore in a nearby lake. This would balance the odds, since both men would be restricted in their movements during the fight. Despite some consternation among the retainers, Shingen quickly agreed to these conditions.

Kansuke and Shingen's vassal were taken out to the anchored boat in another small craft, and they climbed in. Without warning, Kansuke suddenly pierced a hole through the bottom of the boat with the scabbard of his sword, leapt back into the transport craft, and pushed it away. The vassal, who could not swim, now found himself alone in a slowly sinking boat with no way of escape. At this juncture, Kansuke threw the man a rope and pulled him to shore, saving his life.

Watching this affair intently from shore, Shingen quickly fathomed the depth of Kansuke's strategy and immediately retained him, doubling the stipend that had been initially offered.

In this battle, Kansuke had essentially employed three strategies.

First, he had won the battle without fighting, thus protecting his own life. At the same time, he had not injured his opponent, who would now likely become his ally. Finally, before employing the first two strategies, Kansuke had taken into account all of the conditions of the situation: his own physical disabilities, the vassal's simple reliance on his swordsmanship, Shingen's needs and values, and the environment in which the battle would take place. Thus, no blood was shed, and Shingen's highly respected vassal lived to serve him. Kansuke henceforth served as Shingen's respected strategist, helping him to rise as one of the most powerful and feared warlords of his time.

These three concepts are fundamental to Chinese (and subsequently Japanese) military thought, and they run like currents through *The 36 Strategies of the Martial Arts*.

This book consists of thirty-six strategies arranged under six headings, thus mirroring the hexagrams in the *I Ching*, or *Book of Changes*.[3] The original text is quite brief: each strategy is given a title, usually of four Chinese characters, providing the reader with a mnemonic device for the meaning of the following strategy. The strategy itself consists of several lines of classical Chinese, often containing a short phrase from the above-mentioned *Book of Changes*, which may be considered the shadow text of this work. The translation of this strategy appears here in italics at the head of each chapter and is followed by further explanation by Professor Hiroshi Moriya, first a modern rendition, then a more detailed explanation.

In the various editions of this work that have appeared over time, each chapter has been expanded by one or more explanations or illustrations taken from Chinese history. Professor Moriya has followed this precedent, supplying clear and succinct explanations and examples not only from Chinese literature and history but also from events in Europe and modern business affairs, covering a broad spectrum of human activity and conflicts.

The origins of the original 36 *Strategies* are unclear: tradition has cited a certain T'an Tao-chi of the fifth century A.D. as the author, but the text is more likely a synthesis of various military maxims, political expressions, and even folk sayings from over a thousand years before. The sections from the *Book of Changes* date from at least fifteen hundred years before the compilation of the text.

The 36 Strategies of the Martial Arts considers the world as a dynamic field of energy, constantly moving and flowing, in which conditions may call for one strategy now, and another depending upon the changes in the physical and psychological environment. Indeed, an intended strategy may evoke changes itself, and a different strategy may be required as circumstances evolve. Professor Moriya emphasizes time and again that one must avoid rigidity at all costs and be totally aware of the grid of activity and its psychological effects on both one's enemy and oneself. If one cannot meet these requirements, one should leave these strategies alone.

It may be appropriate, then, to think of this book in the way that Confucius described the *Book of Changes* in his amendment, the *Ta chuan*:

> Ah, the *Book of Changes*!
> You should keep it within reach.
> Its Way is frequently shifting,
> Changing and moving without stopping anywhere,
> Flowing through the six Emptinesses,
> While rising and sinking without constancy.
>
> Shifting mutually between the hard and the soft,
> You cannot make it into fixed law;
> It only marches on toward change.

There is, however, a method to its coming and going;
Inside and out, it would have you know apprehension.

It also makes clear sorrow and grief and their causes;
And though you have no great teacher,
You should face it as you would your father and mother.

At first, follow the words, then,
    if you can fathom their direction,
The consistent rules will be there.

But if you are not quite the man [with depth of mind],
The Way will be in vain, and go nowhere.

I owe a great debt of appreciation to Professor Hiroshi Moriya for agreeing to my translating his outstanding work; to my editor, Barry Lancet, for suggesting this project and guiding me through it; to my friend Dr. Daniel Medvedov, for first pointing out to me the inclusion in the text of the lines from the *Book of Changes*; to my mentor, Ichikawa Takashi, for generously providing me with Chinese/Japanese dictionaries and other texts necessary for this project; to my wife Emily, for reading through the translation and rendering it far more readable; and to my late professors Dr. Richard N. McKinnon and Professor Hiraga Noburu, for initially setting my nose to this grindstone with such intelligence, patience, and grace. Any and all mistakes are my own.

William Scott Wilson

INTRODUCTION

Chinese books on the martial arts, which are considered to begin with Sun Tzu's *The Art of War*, regard "winning without fighting" as the most desirable method of victory. In the "Attacking by Stratagem" chapter of his work, for example, a well-known passage perfectly captures this idea:

> To win one hundred battles is not the highest good. The highest good is to have the enemy soldiers submit without fighting.

Why would winning without fighting be so desirable? First, if our forces fight, our own troops will be unable to avoid injury. Second, there is always the possibility that today's enemy may become tomorrow's ally.

So then, how do you win without fighting? Two methods can be considered:

- Confining your opponent's intentions by means of diplomatic negotiations.
- Diminishing your opponent's strength by means of strategy and leading him to internal collapse.

This is essentially winning with strategy rather than by force, or, it might be said, winning with your "head" rather than with your "strength." The Chinese people have favored this method of victory for three thousand years, and they have stored up extensive knowledge in this regard. *The 36 Strategies of the Martial Arts* is, in a sense, a compilation of these methods and teachings.

It is not clear by whom or in what age this book was written. The first source would seem to be the *Nan Ch'i Shu*, a historical work written about fifteen hundred years ago, in which we find, "Of Lord T'an's thirty-six strategies, running away is considered the highest."

This phrase is said to be a judgment upon an incident that occurred when the Ch'i general T'an Tao-chi faced the armies of Wei, a mighty country to the north. He avoided entering into a decisive battle and instead single-mindedly fled in any direction he could. Within this judgment, however, there is a voice that highly praises T'an Tao-chi's manner of battle insofar as he returned with his troops entirely intact.

At any rate, *The 36 Strategies of the Martial Arts* was put together by someone of a later age who took these words about T'an Tao-chi as a cue. The following are the distinctive features concerning its content:

1. There is a natural law for battle. All strategies are based on that natural law and must be investigated thoroughly and rationally.

2. The know-how of battle has been compiled in the historical accounts of the past. You must apply these lessons according to your study of these accounts.

3. The thirty-six strategies compiled here are the essential themes researched by leaders from the past. It would be unforgivable to make light of them.

4. Before putting these strategies into actual practice, it is necessary to clearly diagnose the conditions of both your opponent and yourself. If you apply these strategies blindly while ignoring conditions, you will not be able to avoid failure.

5. When you *do* apply these strategies, do your best to encourage your opponent's carelessness and to discourage him from

wanting to take action. Think in terms of attacking his mind, usurping his energy, and eroding his spirit.

6. Act on natural law to the very end; bear in mind applications that are not unreasonable. You must avoid hit-or-miss risks.

7. When you ascertain that there is no prospect of victory, you should withdraw without hesitation. To be dragged into a quagmire and to suffer a total loss in the end is the most unskillful way of fighting.

I suppose it can be understood that this is a flexible and modest way of thinking. Therefore, it can likely be applied not only to the strategies of war but also as a compass for battle strategies in economics, and even as wise guidance as we conduct ourselves through the passages of life. Indeed, that just may be the greatest appeal of *The 36 Strategies of the Martial Arts*.

In the creation of this book, I consulted the following two works: *Sanshihlu Chi Hsin P'ien*, edited by Li Ping-yen and published by Chan Shih Publishers, and *Sanshihlu Chi*, translated and annotated by Wu Ku and published by Chi Lin Jen Min Publishers.

One final word. This book should not be considered merely information on the ways of the past. I would request strongly that it be read as a book whose practices can enliven our present world.

Hiroshi Moriya

Chronology of
Approximate Dynastic Periods

DYNASTIC PERIOD	YEARS
LEGENDARY SAGE EMPERORS	2852–2255 B.C.
HSIA 2205–1766	
SHANG	1766–1045
CHOU	1045–256
Western Chou	1045–770
Eastern Chou	770–256
Spring and Autumn	722–481
Warring States	403–221
CH'IN	221–206
FORMER HAN	206 B.C.–8 A.D.
LATER HAN	23–220
SIX DYNASTIES	222–589
Three Kingdoms	220–280
Eastern Tsin	317–419
Former Ch'in	351–384
SUI	589–618
T'ANG	618–907
FIVE DYNASTIES	907–959
SUNG	960–1126
SOUTHERN SUNG	1127–1279
YUAN (Mongol)	1279–1368
MING	1368–1644
CH'ING (Manchu)	1644–1911

ANCHOR
ON REALITY

六六三十六、
数中有術、術中有数。
陰陽燮理、機在其中。
機不可設、設則不中。

Six sixes are thirty-six.
In numbers there are techniques.
In techniques there are numbers.
Function resides in the midst of the
harmonious principles of yin and yang.
Function should not be fixed.
If it is fixed, it will not hit the mark.

In the Great Yin hexagram of the *I Ching*, six multiplied by six becomes thirty-six. In the same way, the methods employed for the strategies will be of many kinds and many styles. Strategies are contained within objective laws and therefore must be exercised based on objective laws. If you can grasp the contradictions within reality, you will know how to handle strategies according to the immediate situation. If you act while ignoring reality, you will surely be unable to avoid defeat.

In *The Art of War* there is the phrase "The martial [art] is based on deception." A common saying furthermore states, "The martial [arts] do not abhor deception." "Deception," of course, means to deceive people. Or to put it another way, it is nothing other than to muddle the judgment of the enemy and to impair his vision. Such acts of "deception" are generally called "strategies," "schemes," or "plots."

Methods of employing these thirty-six strategies are innumerable. Every one of them is based on and manifested conclusively by the experiences of men of former times who were real, and who fought real battles. These are not mysterious strategies inspired by the gods.

When putting these strategies into practice, you cannot ignore the real world. When you apply them to the situation at hand, your success will be their warranty.

Part I

STRATEGIES FOR VICTORY IN BATTLE

Even when your own country has superior power, you should not grow confident that the chances of victory reside with your side alone. A moment's negligence can invite an irrevocable defeat. Even during times of peace, you must prudently think over your strategies and aim toward a secure victory.

勝戦の計

Obscure Heaven, Cross the Sea

瞞天過海

備周則意怠、常見則不疑。
陰在陽之內、不在陽之対。
太陽、太陰。

If your preparation is too ambitious,
your attention will be slack.
If you are always looking about [and grow
complacent], you will have no doubts [at
precisely the time you should be having them].
Yin resides inside of yang, not in its
opposition. Great Yang becomes Great Yin.

When you think that your method of defense is
infallible, your vigilance will invariably grow slack.
If you are used to looking at the familiar, you are
liable to harbor no skepticism at times when this is
precisely what you should be harboring.

Clever strategies that are likely to take people
by surprise do not necessarily need to be hidden
from view. They can be hidden in plain sight. Quite
often, secret strategies are hidden in a place where
anyone might see them if they are vigilant enough.

"Obscure Heaven, Cross the Sea" is a strategy by which you show yourself clearly but camouflage your real intentions. You invite your opponent to look on, and when he becomes complacent and thinks you are no longer a threat, you use this advantage to take control and seal your victory.

To begin, you engage in an activity that may or may not be a threat to your opponent. He will not neglect to be vigilant. Then you repeat the activity without initiating any serious action. Again, your opponent will give you his full attention. But after you repeat your action a number of times, your opponent will grow tired of watching and stop considering the activity a threat. With each repetition, he will simply think, "Again?" Then, when you are sure of your opponent's negligence, strike hard and eliminate him. That is the essence of "Obscure Heaven, Cross the Sea." This is simple indeed; but it is a strategy that clearly relies on a blind spot in human psychology, and the possibility of success is high.

◉ The Resourcefulness of T'ai Shih-tz'u

During the period of *The Romance of the Three Kingdoms*,[1] among the wise generals in the employ of Sun Ts'e of Wu was a man by the name of T'ai Shih-tz'u.

This story took place in his younger years. Kung Yung, the prime minister of Pei Hai, was surrounded by a large army of Yellow Cap Rebels[2] at Tu Ch'ang, where his own troops were quartered and now cornered. T'ai Shih-tz'u had formerly received a great favor from Kung Yung, and so immediately hurried to Tu Ch'ang and met with the prime minister.

In their conversation, Kung Yung mentioned that he had wanted to request aid from the nearby country of P'ing Yuan, but the siege of his fortress[3] was heavy, and as passage through enemy lines seemed impossible no one would volunteer to serve as a messenger. At that, T'ai Shih-tz'u thought the time had come for him to repay his debt, and so he volunteered for the job.

The first thing he did was to fortify himself with a meal and wait for dawn. Then, grabbing his whip and his bow, he leapt onto his horse and, accompanied by twelve men carrying targets, opened the fortress gate and dashed outside. The rebel soldiers who had encircled the fortress were taken by surprise. Thrown into confusion, they brought out their horses and prepared to prevent the man's escape.

But T'ai Shih-tz'u casually got down from his horse, entered the trench beside the fortress, set the targets up, and nonchalantly began to practice archery. Then, when he had shot all his arrows, he returned to the fortress.

The next day he went out again for archery practice. This time, while some of the rebel soldiers stood up and remained vigilant, there were also some who, convinced this time there was no threat, laid down and ignored the spectacle. T'ai Shih-tz'u set up the targets and, when he was finished shooting, withdrew to the fortress.

When this happened a third time, the rebel soldiers had grown so complacent they simply thought, "Again?" and not one of them rose to stand vigil. T'ai Shih-tz'u waited carefully for his moment, then suddenly whipped his horse and broke through the encircling net.

Soon after that, reinforcements arrived from P'ing Yuan.

⊛ The Strategy of Ho Jo-pi

The Sui-dynasty general Ho Jo-pi also employed a visual illusion to deceive his enemy. It was the end of the period of the Northern and Southern Courts (two separate dynasties preceding the Sui) when the Sui dynasty destroyed the Ch'en. The Sui made their capital at Ch'ang-an, taking possession of the territory north of the Yangtze River. In contrast, the Ch'en had made their capital at Chien-yeh and had possession of the lands south of the river. Therefore, if the Sui were to attack the Ch'en, they would have to cross the Yangtze.

General Ho Jo-pi's problem was how to put his enemy off their game, so he devised a ruse.

First, when the corps of Sui troops that had been placed along the Yangtze on the bank opposite to Chien-yeh were due to return home, the general had them gather on the outskirts of the village of Li-yang, hoist a forest of banners, and give the appearance of a great concentrated army. Alarmed, the Ch'en troops mobilized and consolidated their defense on the other side of the river.

The Sui troops never crossed the river. Instead, the corps rotated out and returned home.

This action was repeated three times. The Ch'en soldiers came to believe that the massing of troops at that point of the river was not a threatening military maneuver. They stopped taking the event seriously and no longer made any special preparations in response.

The deception succeeded wonderfully. When the Sui troops *did* cross the river and attack, they were met with almost no organized resistance, and they captured Chien-yeh with ease.

⊛ Retreat Seven Times

During the Spring and Autumn period, King[4] Chuang of Ch'u attacked Yung. His advance troops made an incursion close to the capital of Yung, but at that juncture the enemy made a counterattack, causing the advance troops to flee and return home.

Someone in the Ch'u camp, analyzing the situation, said, "Yung not only has great military strength but they are adding vast numbers of barbarian troops to their force. If we were to attack them now, there would be no chance of victory. I think that we should wait until our main force arrives and then attack."

But the commanding officer of the advance troops replied, "That's no good at all. We'll continue to fight just as we are, but then purposely make as though we're retreating. No doubt our opponents will be taken in by this and become negligent. This will gain us some advantage."

This said, he continued his attacks. Seven times he fought and seven times he retreated. Seeing this, the Yung generals said, "These Ch'u troops! They have the nerve to contend with us, but they are absolute fools!" and made no proper efforts to tighten their security.

At that point, the main force of troops commanded by King Chuang arrived. The Ch'u forces attacked for the eighth time, this time without retreating, and destroyed the Yung with ease.

Had the commanding officer of the Ch'u not chosen to attack and withdraw as many times as he had, the Yung would have met the main force of King Chuang with their own best effort. As it was, they no longer believed in the fortitude of the Ch'u troops and were caught completely off guard, thus insuring the brilliant strategic victory of the Ch'u.

◉ Hitler's Lightning Strike

"Obscure Heaven, Cross the Sea" was not just applied in the distant past. During World War II, for example, Hitler's lightning attack against France made use of the strategy.

Hitler secretly leaked his scheduled day of attack to the Allies, and when he saw that they were alarmed and had prepared an opposing force, the Nazi leader simply changed the scheduled day. This he did repeatedly over the following weeks. Each time the Allies prepared their defenses and each time Hitler changed the scheduled day of attack. The Allies grew weary of Hitler's endless changes and decided that the German leader was simply waging "a war of nerves." Gradually, the Allies allowed their vigilance to slacken.

Hitler broke through the Maginot Line and surged into French territory on May 14, 1940. At the time, the intelligence corps of France and England correctly identified the movement of the German troops, yet the governments of both countries regarded the latest piece of intelligence as simply another stage in Hitler's war of nerves and paid little attention. This would prove a grave error: their inaction greatly aided the success of Hitler's lightning strike.

SURROUND WEI, HELP CHAO

囲魏救趙

共敵不如分敵。
敵陽不如敵陰。

*When facing your enemies, there is nothing
like dividing them.
For the yang of an enemy, there is nothing
like his yin.*

Rather than launch an attack on a powerful enemy,
it is better first to disperse his military strength and
that of his allies, and then attack.

Rather than attack the enemy first, it is better to
wait for him to make a move, and then gain control.

"Surround Wei, Help Chao" was a strategy employed during the period of Warring States when Sun Pin, a tactician for the state of Ch'i, came to the aid of Chao by attacking the army of Wei in a roundabout manner. From the very beginning, and especially in the case of an enemy with a huge force, it is unwise to confront him head-on, since the probability of a victory would be extremely low. Furthermore, even if a smaller army *were* momentarily blessed with good luck and managed to win, the damage to its troops would be severe.

If direct confrontation is best avoided, then what kind of strategy should be used against a powerful enemy?

"Controlling an army is like controlling water." That is to say, the way of engaging in battle is by and large the same as the way of controlling a flood. It is, for example, difficult to get close to a raging, roiling current. But if you can disperse the current and cause it to flow into a number of different channels, you can weaken its power until it becomes manageable.

In the same way, when opposing an overwhelming opponent, you must first divide his forces and wear him down. If you were then to attack, it would be much easier to defeat him.

To the very end, you must avoid confronting him head-on, but rather divide and then attack. This is essence of "Surround Wei, Help Chao."

⊚ Sun Pin's Twofold Victory

During the period of Warring States, Wei mobilized its great army and laid siege to Han Tan, the capital of Chao. Chao was unable to resist the ferocious attack of the Wei army, and it asked for aid from the state of Ch'i. Ch'i sent reinforcements, appointing the chief vassal T'ien Chi as commanding general and the military strategist Sun Pin as tactician.

As soon as T'ien Chi took up his post, he immediately led the army toward Han Tan, planning to attack, arguably a perfectly sensible strategy. However, the tactician Sun Pin voiced an objection.

"When you untangle a thread," Sun Pin said, "you don't pull at it indiscriminately. Likewise, when you assist someone in a fight, if you exchange blows indiscriminately you'll be unable to control the situation. Rather, it is better to strike at your opponent's weakness to gain an advantage over the situation. At this point in the fight, Wei has thrown all of its best troops into the battle with Chao, and only old and weak soldiers remain in the state itself. Now is the time to strike the weakened capital of Wei. If we do this, Wei will be forced to lift its siege of Han Tan and return its troops to its home state. This strategy kills two birds with one stone: it will not only cause our opponent to lift his siege but will also weaken him on the home front at the same time."

T'ien Chi thought the strategy reasonable and put it into action. Upon learning of the impending attack on their capital, the Wei army left Han Tan and hastily took the road home in order to repel the Ch'i.

The Ch'i army attacked the Wei at Kuei Ling and gained a great victory.

◉ How Mao Tse-tung Harassed the Japanese Army

History may accuse Mao Tse-tung of any number of failures in his later years, but when he led the Eighth Route Army and fought the Japanese, he devised some marvelous military strategies and tactics and harassed the Japanese troops no end. One of his favorite strategies was a variation of "Surround Wei, Help Chao." In a document entitled *Questions on Guerrilla Warfare in Resisting Japan*, he stated the following:

> In a plan of military operations for resisting a siege, our major strength is generally placed in an interior line. Nevertheless, on the basis of conditions where we have a full margin of strength,

we should use a secondary force in an exterior line, and there break the enemy's line of communication and restrain his reinforcements. If the enemy remains in his headquarters for a long time and shows no indication of moving, our troops use the reverse of the above-mentioned method. That is to say, we leave a division of troops within the vicinity of his headquarters to surround him, but with the main force attack an area where he has trespassed. This will push him into great activity, and the troops that had remained for a long time around their headquarters will now leave in order to attack our main force. This is the method of "Surround Wei, Help Chao."

The Japanese army drank many a bitter cup from this mobile military tactic and eventually lost the upper hand.

⊛ Economic Strategies for Minor Enterprises That Can Be Learned from *The Art of War*

The concentration of allies and dispersion of the enemy is a military tactic stressed in Sun Tzu's *The Art of War*. In this book it says:

> While we temporarily concentrate our troops into one, the enemy is dispersed into ten. In this case, the strength of ten separate entities confronts the strength of one. In other words, our troops have a great force while the enemy has none at all. When you meet no force with a great force, your opponent will be disposed of easily.
>
> Therefore, if the enemy defends what is in front of him, what is behind him will be weak; if he defends what is behind him, what is in front of him will be weak. If he defends his left, his right will be weak; if he defends his right, his left will be weak. If he defends himself in every direction, every direction will be weak.

The measure of military strength never exceeds relative conditions. If you can divide the enemy and then attack, you will be able to advance in the battle with the advantage.

This way of thinking may also be applicable to economic tactics for small businesses. The minor enterprise of "lesser military strength" will not survive if it tries to take on larger enterprises and attempts to muscle in on their territory. In order to survive it must concentrate its martial strength, plan the development of its own unique product, and strike at an opening or gap in a business of larger size.

Strategy *3*

Borrow
a Sword to
Make Your Kill

借刀殺人

敵已明、友未定、
引友殺敵、不自出刀、
以損推演。

When your enemy is already known,
but your allies are still uncertain,
draw your allies into killing your enemy.
Do not brandish a sword yourself.
Draw your conclusion by the damage done.

Even though the enemy has set his battle plans in
motion, you may not yet have determined the attitude of your own allies. At such a time, tempt your
allies to attack the enemy, but keep your own troops
in reserve. This is nothing other than the practical application of the 41st chapter of the *I Ching*,
"Damage": "The inferior suffers damage; the superior increases."

There are two sides to "Borrow a Sword to Make Your Kill." One calls for you to curb your own activity while convincing a third party to destroy your enemy. To use a common Japanese saying, you could "win at sumo with the other person's loincloth." This allows you to defeat the enemy and still preserve your own force without change.

Yet this is just the beginning. At a higher level, you do not rely on a third party to attack your enemy but rather cause him to turn his own strength upon himself. This strategy creates a splitting maneuver that cleverly uses the enemy's own power to weaken his position, eventually driving him to collapse. This is the very core of "Borrow a Sword to Make Your Kill."

⊛ How Ts'ao Ts'ao Used Sun Ch'uan's Sword

The Romance of the Three Kingdoms took place during a time when Ts'ao Ts'ao of Wei, Liu Pei of Shu, and Sun Ch'uan of Wu[1] were confronting each other for the control of China. With three powerful rivals vying for hegemony, the strategy of "Borrow a Sword to Make Your Kill" often came into play. The following episode is but one example:

Kuan Yu,[2] one of Liu Pei's commanders, mobilized a large army, attacked the territory of the Wei, and laid siege to the fortress at Fan. Ts'ao Ts'ao sent reinforcements, but they were utterly annihilated by Kuan Yu's counterattack. Now, if Fan fell to Kuan Yu, Wei's capital Hsu would be in great danger. In fear of Kuan Yu's forces, Ts'ao Ts'ao seemed flustered and ready to relocate his capital to a safer territory farther away. At this point, the strategist and counselor Sze Ma Chung-ta approached Ts'ao Ts'ao with these words:

"We should bring Sun Ch'uan into action here, as he also has good reason to fear the swelling of Kuan Yu's forces. Divide Kuan Yu's territory and offer the land south of the Yangtze to Sun Ch'uan. Under that condition, request him to dispatch troops and strike at Kuan Yu's rear. If he does this, the siege of the fortress will not be worth Kuan Yu's effort, and he will withdraw."

Convinced of the soundness of this strategy, Ts'ao Ts'ao immediately dispatched a messenger to Sun Ch'uan proposing his cooperation.

Sun Ch'uan embraced the idea of striking at Kuan Yu and extending his lands. He mobilized his troops and captured Chiang Lu, Kuan Yu's home base. Kuan Yu was compelled to end his siege of the fortress at Fan, but with his home base lost he was easily captured and killed.

For his part, Ts'ao Ts'ao had successfully employed the strategy of "Borrow a Sword to Make Your Kill." With little expenditure, he gained territory and vanquished an enemy, using an alliance with Sun Ch'uan to force Kuan Yu to destroy himself.

⊛ Borrowing from the Enemy

This story appears in the *Han Fei Tzu*:[3]

During the Spring and Autumn period, Huai Kung, the ruler of the state of Cheng, wanted to invade the state of Kuai and make it his own. Even though Kuai was a small state and would not be able to resist a frontal assault for long, the people of Kuai would probably defend their home for all they were worth, which would result in a considerable loss of blood on both sides. Knowing this, Huai Kung searched for a plan to undermine his opponent's resistance.

First, Kung drew up a list of Kuai's strongest warriors and leaders. Next, he wrote letters to each of them promising more land and appealing new posts in return for their support. Then one night, Kung constructed an altar near the fortress gate of Kuai, buried the letters and list, and poured the blood of roosters and pigs over the spot when he had buried them. (In those days, when either states or individuals entered into a pledge, tradition called for them to slaughter pigs and roosters and then mutually sip the sacrificial blood.)

The following morning the ruler of Kuai discovered this "evidence." Believing he had been betrayed, he ordered the execution of every vassal that appeared on the list. With Kuai's most able men eliminated, Huai Kung promptly invaded and conquered the state of Kuai without difficulty.

⚙ Hitler's Ploy

Recent times have produced good examples of this strategy, even though you might think that such a transparent, wedge-driving ploy would no longer be effective.

Before World War II, there was a very able Soviet general by the name of Marshal Tohachevski. In 1938, when Stalin set a purge in motion, rumor suggested that Tohachevski, too, might be caught up in the sweep. If an able general like Tohachevski were purged, it would be of great benefit to Germany. Therefore, Hitler took the opportunity to bury the man. Calling in the head of the German intelligence agency, he secretly ordered the man to fabricate treasonous documents incriminating Tohachevski.

The officer created a packet of documents that included private messages passed between Tohachevski's group and German generals. The pack also included lists of the circumstances under which Tohachevski and his friends had sold information to the Germans, along with the amounts of money they received in return, and copies of replies sent to Tohachevski from the German intelligence agency.

In an additional stroke of brilliance, the German intelligence officer made the information extremely hard to procure. The Soviet Union eventually bought the phony document packet for the enormous sum of three million rubles, and based on its disclosures arrested eight generals, including Tohachevski. In the eyes of Stalin's inquisitioners, the sheer volume of the so-called evidence made it nearly impossible for the generals to refute, and after just a few minutes of questioning Tohachevski and the others were sentenced to death. Within twelve hours, every one of them had been executed.

Hitler's borrowed sword was a spectacular success.

⊛ The Soviet Union's Diplomatic Strategy

At a roundtable discussion, Kase Shun'ichi, a commentator on international relations, told the following story about Soviet diplomatic strategy:

"I sometimes read Chinese poetry, and think that this 'Borrow a Sword to Make Your Kill' strategy is a 'shop specialty' of the Soviet Union. The most typical example of this was the German-Soviet non-aggression pact. Hitler was made to think that Russia, which was at his back, was secure, and so he turned his attention toward France and England. He then invaded Poland, which touched off the war in Europe. After that, Stalin concluded a neutrality pact with Japan, thereby encouraging Japan to march south, and this eventually led to fighting between Japan and the United States, commencing of course with Pearl Harbor. I imagine this was also a clever use of the strategy."

In other words, by taking themselves out of the fray, the Soviets forced others to tackle Hitler's growing military machine. Of course, the strategy may not be an exclusive specialty of Soviet diplomacy, for surely we can see that the diplomatic machinations of many countries contain aspects of this strategy. It is simply a matter of how audaciously a country's leaders choose to use it. In any case, let overly optimistic leaders ignore the strategy at their own peril.

One last note. This stratagem is not confined to diplomatic circles and warring states. It has found an equally comfortable home in the relations between individuals as well.

AWAIT HIS TIRED STEPS AT YOUR LEISURE

以逸待劳

困敵之勢、不以戰、
損剛益柔。

To afflict damage on the enemy's forces,
do not rely on battle;
decrease the hard, increase the soft.[1]

To pursue your enemy successfully, it is not absolutely necessary to intensify your attack. If you consolidate your defense and encourage the enemy's fatigue, you can transform your own stance from one of inferiority to superiority.

The strategy of "Await His Tired Steps at Your Leisure" seeks to increase your troops' leisure (and thus refresh them), allowing them to keep their composure while awaiting the enemy's fatigue. In the "The Hollow and the Real" chapter of Sun Tzu's *The Art of War*, it says:

> If you proceed to the battlefield before the enemy and intercept him, you will be able to fight with composure. If, on the contrary, you arrive at the battlefield after the enemy, you will be forced into a difficult fight. Thus, if you are skillful in battle, you will not be drawn into the strategies and maneuvers of the enemy.

In the "Maneuvering" chapter, it continues:

> Take up a position in a beneficial location, and await the enemy's coming from afar. Be fully rested, and await the enemy's fatigue; eat to satiety, and await the enemy's starvation.

Although the word "await" suggests a certain passiveness, this does not mean that you should await good fortune or a fortuitous act of Heaven. Rather, this strategy requires the active nourishing of an ardor to strike at the enemy without remiss, to preserve and protect one's strength, and to await the enemy's fatigue while fortifying your own reserves. Then, grasping the moment when the enemy appears to be exhausted, press forward with singular resolve and take the victory.

"Await His Tired Steps at Your Leisure" is essentially a strategy for grasping the initiative in battle by wearing down your opponent in a subtle manner.

⊛ Sun Pin Defeats the Wei Troops a Second Time

Thirteen years after the Ch'i tactician Sun Pin defeated the troops of Wei with the strategy of "Surround Wei, Help Chao," he again demolished the Wei army, this time with the strategy of "Await His Tired Steps at Your Leisure."

The year was 341 B.C. by the Western calendar, and Wei had mobilized a large army to attack the state of Han. Receiving an urgent request to come to Han's aid, Ch'i once again appointed T'ien Chi as commanding general, and once again he had his troops attack the Wei capital at Ta Liang.

The Wei general, P'ang Chuan, was determined not to fall into the same trap twice. Turning his army around, this time he took up a position to attack the Ch'i army from the rear. At this point, the tactician Sun Pin suggested the following to T'ien Chi:

"The Wei soldiers are reckless at heart and believe our troops to be cowardly. The person who fights well is one who can make use of his enemy's spirit in reverse. And in the martial arts it is said that when you are enticed by gain and chase the enemy too far, you will lose your general in a hundred leagues, and half your soldiers in fifty. Let us gradually decrease the number of our campfires when we billet from one hundred thousand today to fifty thousand tomorrow, and then to thirty thousand the day after."

P'ang Chuan saw that the campfires of the Ch'i army were decreasing, and on the third day of the pursuit he rejoiced. "I've heard that the Ch'i troops were cowards, but they've been in our territory barely three days, and already more than half of them have deserted. This is incredible!"

So saying, he left his foot soldiers behind and, leading only a light cavalry, began what he expected would be a quick and sure defeat.

Meanwhile, Sun Pin had estimated that the approaching Wei troops would reach Ma Ling around the evening. Ma Ling was in a ravine. The road in was narrow, and steep slopes bounded both sides. Thus it was the perfect place for an ambush.

P'ang Chuan's cavalry approached Ma Ling. All of a sudden, the crossbows of the Ch'i troops sang out with one voice. As darkness descended, the Wei troops fell into great disorder and were destroyed.

In the midst of the battle, P'ang Chuan is said to have committed suicide. Sun Pin had consolidated his defense and chosen the battlefield well. In inviting his enemy's approach he had abandoned the hard for the soft, and was able to strike with a single blow at his fully extended opponent, making for an overwhelming victory.

✸ Lu Sun's Manipulation of Troops

During the period of the Three Kingdoms, Wu's commanding general, Lu Sun, won a resounding victory by using this strategy at the Battle of I-ling against the great army of Liu Pei.

Upon hearing of Liu Pei's dispatch of troops, all of the commanders of the Wu army grew agitated and prepared for battle. The supreme commander, Lu Sun, calmed his generals and said, "Liu Pei has mobilized his entire army and has made an incursion into our territory. Moreover, as he has camped in a natural stronghold, we cannot attack and defeat him. And even if we attacked him successfully, we would be unable to destroy his entire army. If we lost, we would be inviting an irrevocable situation. On the other hand, our troops' morale will not weaken if we wait here for a little while. We can assess the situation and maybe change it, making arrangements to our advantage. The enemy is advancing through the mountains, so their troops will arrive fatigued. We, meanwhile, can sit here happily and await the exhaustion of their troops."

Lu Sun's thinking aligned perfectly with the strategy "Await His Tired Steps at Your Leisure," but the other generals could not understand his suggestion. They whispered among themselves that Lu Sun was losing his nerve.

But the fact was that Liu Pei's exhausted army was in no condition to fight. In a drawn-out battle, his road-weary troops would be at a great disadvantage. This was unavoidable. Aware of the problem, Liu

Pei added several thousand additional troops, had them encamp on level ground, thus inviting the Wu army to make its attack. The Wu generals thought that now, indeed, was their chance, and scrambled together in a unified force. Lu Sun, however, held them back yet again, saying, "Wait a while. They are undoubtedly setting a trap."

In this way, both armies patiently stood their ground for over half a year. Finally, it was apparent that Liu Pei's side, which was unable to initiate a strike against the Wu troops on higher ground, was growing fatigued. At last, frustrated with the stalemate, Lu Sun gathered his generals together and commanded them to make preparations for the attack.

The generals disagreed. "We should have struck their vanguard earlier. Now, over half a year has elapsed, and during that time the enemy has captured a great number of positions that he guards forcefully. Even if we were to attack now, we would have no chance of victory."

Lu Sun, however, said that this was not the case. "Don't you see that Liu Pei is an old campaigner of many battles? When he first approached, he had a detailed plan, so had we fought then, we would have had no chance of victory. But now, his line of battle is at a standstill, his troops' fatigue is at its height, and they are demoralized. Even more importantly, he has no plan to resolve his problem. Now, indeed, is our best chance to surround and annihilate him."

So saying, he made an all-out attack and, after much fierce fighting, destroyed Liu Pei's great army.

⊛ Master Kimura

Shogi Master Kimura Yoshio, who raised an entire generation on the game of *shogi*, used "Await His Tired Steps at Your Leisure" as a weapon in his arsenal of tactics. Generally speaking, long periods of thought in *shogi* competition indicate an unfavorable turn of events. However, Master Kimura turned this technique on its head. Rather than dropping into deep thought when his own situation grew precarious, he would sink into deep periods of thought whenever his competitors' circumstances grew unfavorable. Many of them were unable to endure this Kimura's "long thinking." They grew impatient and their spirits sank, which was of course Master Kimura's intention. For all we know, he could have been thinking about what he was going to have for dinner as he watched his opponent's expression with a faraway look. But his tactics were successful. As a result, half of his opponents would resign in defeat rather than continue in an attempt to draw victory from a weaker but not insurmountable position.

Take Advantage of the Fire to Plunder the Goods

趁火打劫

敵之害大、就勢取利。
剛決柔也。

If the enemy's injury is great, attack with force, and profit.
The hard will scatter the soft.[1]

When you drive the enemy into desperate circumstances, you must attack him overwhelmingly and bring the matter to an end with a single blow. This is a strategy in which the strong takes advantage of his own power and vanquishes a weak enemy.

"Take Advantage of the Fire to Plunder the Goods" is fundamentally a strategy in which you take advantage of a person's weaker position to force yourself in and commit larceny. That is to say, you take advantage of your opponent's weakness to attack him mercilessly. If your opponent's forces are firmly united and have prepared for an invasion, your attack will not easily succeed. On the other hand, if your opponent is hamstrung by factional strife, or the common people are beaten down by dissatisfaction with their lives, or he is distressed by pressure from the outside, you have an unparalleled opportunity. At such times, you should strike unhesitatingly and finish him off completely. This is the strategy of "Take Advantage of the Fire to Plunder the Goods."

But what do you do in situations when you are unable to discover an opening with which to take advantage of your opponent? Two countermeasures can be considered. The first is to wait patiently until your opponent exposes a weak side. The other is to induce your opponent to expose his vulnerable spot.

◉ Liu Pang Defeats Hsiang Yu

With the death of the First Emperor,[2] the Ch'in dynasty fell, and two outstanding men, Liu Pang[3] and Hsiang Yu,[4] took the opportunity to fight for the hegemony of China. The clash between these two heroes has been called the Battle of Ch'u and Han. The battle continued for over three years. In the beginning, Hsiang Yu's superior military force held sway. Liu Pang fought and was defeated, regrouped and fought and lost again, and was continually chased away each time he regrouped.

Throughout all of this, however, Liu Pang fought with tenacity and gradually gained ground. By the third year of battle, Liu Pang's strategic ascendancy was beginning to take hold, and Hsiang Yu grew increasingly more isolated. However, after three years of intense fighting, Liu Pang's forces were also burdened with fatigue.

In this state of affairs, consequent to an offer made by Liu Pang, both sides agreed to an armistice. Hsiang Yu immediately headed home, and Liu Pang also prepared to collect and withdraw his troops.

At this point, the tacticians Chang Liang and Ch'en P'ing advanced and spoke to Liu Pang one after the other.

"Not only do we possess one-half of the empire, but the local lords have also become your allies. Hsiang Yu's military strength is spent and his supplies are low. This indeed is proof that Heaven has forsaken Hsiang Yu. If you do not take this opportunity to attack him, it will be nothing other than 'nurturing a tiger and planting the seeds of disaster.'"

The root of this idea was, of course, to "Take Advantage of the Fire to Plunder the Goods." The tacticians reasoned that if Liu Pang did not finish off his enemy now, it would be impossible to know when he would have another opportunity. In short, Liu Pang should take advantage of his opponent's weakness and strike him down.

Liu Pang agreed, prepared a carefully arranged incursion, moved his troops in pursuit, and finally destroyed Hsiang Yu.

⊛ The "Human-heartedness" of Sung Huai

In contrast to Liu Pang's decisive action, Huai Kung, the ruler of Sung, took pity on his enemy and let a perfect opportunity pass. He showed *jin*, or "human-heartedness."

During the Spring and Autumn period, Ch'u mobilized a large army with plans to attack Sung. The Sung troops prepared to meet the enemy along the banks of the Hung River. On that day, the Sung were ready for battle, had taken up their positions, and were awaiting the Ch'u army. The Ch'u troops, however, had not even finished crossing the river, let alone taken up a position.

Seeing this, the army commander, Mu I, advanced and spoke to Huai Kung:

"The enemy has a greater force, and our allies are few. They have not yet crossed the river. Let's attack them before they are fully prepared."

But Huai Kung said, "No, no. I'm not capable of such cowardice," and turned a deaf ear to Mu I's advice.

Not long after, the Ch'u army crossed the river and began to set up their battle formation. Mu I again recommended an attack, but again Huai Kung refused, saying, "No, only after they've prepared their battle formation."

The outcome was predictable. Once both armies were fully prepared, the Sung army was unsparingly routed. Huai Kung himself received a leg wound, and in the end his forces collapsed and took flight.

It is said that people of the time derisively referred to Huai Kung's sympathy and consideration for the enemy as "Sung Huai's 'human-heartedness.'"

◉ Give the Enemy an Opening and He Will Take Advantage of It

There is a passage in *The Book of Poetry*[5] that goes, "Brothers may fight inside the wall but will guard against their enemy outside." That is, even though brother may fight brother inside the house, they will rally to a unified line of defense when attacked from the outside.

This is the ideal, to be sure, but it is often not the reality. How many times has a family come to complete ruin as a result of brother fighting brother? The same is true of nations and businesses. Internal antagonisms, internal disputes—all such things weaken organizational strength and invite a reduction of achievement.

But even that would be tolerable if there weren't opponents in the shadows just waiting for an opening. Should there be such an opponent, he will take advantage of a situation without hesitation.

The Soviet Union's invasion of Afghanistan in 1979 is a prime example of this. Regardless of the outcome of the conflict or your personal opinion on the subject, clearly one reason the Soviets invaded in the first place was because the Afghans left them an opening too tempting to ignore.

If an opening is given, it will be taken advantage of. Therefore, one should protect one's position by not showing any vulnerability, especially when one's position is not entirely secure.

Strategy **6**

BE HEARD IN THE EAST, ATTACK FROM THE WEST

声東擊西

敵志乱萃、不虞、
坤下兌上之象。
利其不自主而取之。

Disturb the enemy's focus.
If he is unable to think straight, you will
have the image of the hexagram,
Ts'ui, the Earth below, the Lake above
[the breakthrough of rising water].
Take advantage of his being unable to
manage on his own and seize control.[1]

When the enemy's line of command is in confusion due to an attack, he may become distracted and be unable to respond properly to changes in circumstances. This is similar to the situation of an imminent break in an embankment when the water rises to a threatening level. At such a time, you must take advantage of the enemy's confusion and annihilate him with a single blow.

"Be Heard in the East, Attack from the West" comprises the following steps:

- First, develop a feint operation by appearing to strike from a direction other than your intended goal.
- The enemy will be forced to shift his troops to strengthen his defenses in the area of the attack, leaving other areas more vulnerable.
- Strike immediately at the weakened area.

The source of this strategy may be the ninth-century encyclopedia *T'ung Tien,* which says, "Raise your voice as though striking in the east, but in reality, strike in the west."

This strategy relies on illusion to confuse or trick the enemy. The key is to pull the enemy into a feint operation and have him commit a considerable size of his army so as to weaken his force at the real point of attack. However, if the enemy commander retains his composure and judgment, or clearly reads what you have in store for him, he will most likely set up a countertactic. This strategy must be employed convincingly and with the cunning of your adversary foremost in mind. If you fail in this and are outmaneuvered, you will surely suffer a significant defeat. Therefore, employ this tactic when you find a level of incompetence in the enemy's commander and/or confusion in his line of command.

⊛ Ts'ao Ts'ao Counters Yuan Shao

The climax of the first half of *The Romance of the Three Kingdoms* was the Battle of Kuan Tu, when Ts'ao Ts'ao and Yuan Shao clashed over the hegemony of northern China. Yuan Shao, leading a large army of one hundred thousand men, attacked Ts'ao Ts'ao's headquarters at Hsu, first dispatching his advance troops to surround Ts'ao Ts'ao's advance base at Bai Ma. That they were able to envelope Bai Ma so easily affected the morale of all the troops. Ts'ao Ts'ao himself led his main force, intending to hasten to the relief of the surrounded town. Just then, a staff officer by the name of Hsun Yu advanced and said:

"There is no way we can defeat him with sheer military force. We must find a means to break up the enemy's military strength. We need a two-step plan. First, send a part of our army toward Yen Chin, cross the Yellow River, and make the pretense of circling around to the enemy's rear. This will cause Yuan Shao to move a part of his large army to the west in order to meet our attack. With this opening, lead a light cavalry to Bai Ma and quickly strike at the enemy in a surprise attack. If you do this, you can destroy him."

Ts'ao Ts'ao chose to follow the advice. As soon as Yuan Shao heard that Ts'ao Ts'ao's troops had crossed the river at Yen Chin and were closing in for an attack, he immediately divided his army in half and led one of the divisions to meet the attack. When Ts'ao Ts'ao ascertained the split, he swiftly withdrew his entire army and hurried to Bai Ma, where he utterly destroyed the other division of Yuan Shao's army and eliminated the threat to his advance base.

⊛ Guerrilla Warfare and "Be Heard in the East, Attack from the West"

The guerrilla tactics of the Eighth Route Army led by Mao Tse-tung often employed this strategy. In his famous *Comments on Protracted Warfare*, Mao Tse-tung stated the following:

> Superior force and leadership may fall due to illusion and inattentiveness. Therefore, creating an illusion to fool the enemy and take him by surprise is the way to overcome superior forces and take the lead. What is illusion? "To feint striking in the east while truly striking in the west" is one way of creating illusion. In situations where there is an excellent popular base that will protect information leaks, and one can take various methods for deceiving the enemy, you can often trick the enemy into making

mistakes in both judgment and action. If so, you may be able to rob your enemy of his superior force and leadership position.

It is common knowledge that the Japanese army fell victim to Mao's feints and found itself frustrated and its position weakened.

"Be Heard in the East, Attack from the West" is a classic technique, and one should fully understand that it is readily available to both enemy and ally. But even then, if its execution is skillful, the results will be astonishing. To this day, this technique has not lost its effectiveness.

⊛ Napoleon's Strategy for Embarkation to Egypt

In 1798, when the French fleet led by Napoleon wanted to leave the port of Toulon and embark to Egypt, it faced a major hurdle: the formidable British fleet, led by Admiral Nelson, controlled the Mediterranean Sea. In order to make his way, Napoleon needed to force his opponent to move. To do so, he employed "Be Heard in the East, Attack from the West."

When Napoleon had made all his preparations to depart Toulon, he sent out information that the object of his campaign would be Ireland, in the opposite direction beyond the Straits of Gibraltar. Thinking the plan perfectly plausible, Nelson fell for the ruse and gathered the British fleet close to Gibraltar, waiting for a confrontation.

Napoleon's ploy had worked, and he was able to swiftly take advantage of the opening created by the redeployment of the British fleet, and embark for Egypt.

If the execution is skillful, even a great admiral like Nelson can be drawn in.

Part II

STRATEGIES FOR ENGAGING THE ENEMY

When you engage in hostilities against the enemy, you must not show any weakness. While your troops display their strength, take advantage of the enemy's weakness and plan the extension of your base. You must intend to engage your enemy in a fight in which you attack his weakness with your strength. Let him cut your skin, while you cut through his flesh.

敵戦の計

CREATE EXISTENCE FROM NONEXISTENCE

無中生有

誑也。

非誑也。

実其所誑也。

少陰、太陰、太陽。

There is deception.
There is other than deception.
Place your strength in deception.
Small yin grows to great yin,
and in turn to great yang.

You confound the enemy's vision by making it appear as though something exists, even though it does not. However, it is difficult to pass this deception off to the very end, so you must finally switch over and make sure something *does* come from nothing. In short, you conceal the true form in a provisional one and ensnare the enemy in an illusion.

"Create Existence from Nonexistence" is a strategy in which you create an illusion of existence, and so confuse your opponent's judgment. The following two conditions are prerequisites for making this strategy a success:

- The enemy commander must be the type of person who will easily fall for the strategy you have devised, whether he be simple-minded or suspicious.
- If your illusion confuses the enemy's judgment, in the next step you change to "existence," then follow up with a rain of blows in one single effort.

The change from nonexistence to existence, or from "emptiness" to "reality," is the secret to success.

⊕ Chang Hsun's Straw Mannequins

During the T'ang period, An Lu-shan rose in rebellion and ordered his general, Ling Ku-ch'ao, to surround the fortress at Yung Ch'in. At this time, a man by the name of Chang Hsun was given the responsibility of commanding the garrison. The rebel forces were strong, and the garrison was quickly isolated and cut off from all relief.

At that point, Chang Hsun devised a tactic to break through their predicament. He ordered his soldiers to make a thousand mannequins of straw, dress them in black clothing, secure them with rope, and lower them down the fortress walls at night. Seeing the mannequins, the rebel soldiers thought that men were descending the walls, and so rushed to the forefront and unleashed a torrent of arrows. Chang Hsun's men raised the straw dummies and successfully harvested thousands of arrows, thus refreshing their supply.

The next night Chang Hsun once again ordered the dummies to be lowered. This time the rebel forces unleashed only a few arrows before they drew back.

On the third night, Chang Hsun lowered his soldiers down the walls. The enemy forces refused to be fooled a third time and simply laughed as they watched the descent from a distance, making no preparations for battle.

In this way Chang Hsun successfully lowered five hundred soldiers down the fortress walls, caught the enemy by surprise with this suicide corps, and struck the enemy down without mercy.

⊛ How Fu Chien Brought About His Own Defeat

The end of the fourth century was the era of the Eastern Tsin court, which had its capital in Nan Ching. Fu Chien of the Former Ch'in held sway over all of northern China, and in order to destroy the Eastern Tsin and unite the entire country, he mobilized a great army of one million men and advanced for an attack. The Eastern Tsin army that came to meet the attack was composed of fewer than eighty thousand men, less than one-tenth the size of its opponent.

The two armies clashed along the banks of the Fei River, and the result, contrary to the general expectation, ended in a huge victory for the smaller army. Why was this overwhelmingly superior force defeated and put to flight? The key is in the terror that was induced from an illusion perpetrated by the Eastern Tsin on Fu Chien.

The inferior force of the Eastern Tsin army took the initiative and opened a concerted attack. From the very outset, Fu Chien made little of his opponent's military strength. However, when he took a closer look, his opponent was approaching in a battle formation so tight, so impressive, that it appeared even water could not have passed through. Frightened, Fu Chien did not stop to think, and fell under the mistaken perception that the troops of the Eastern Tsin stretched far into the distance, all the way to the foot of Mount Pa Kung. He turned to his staff officers and muttered, "This is incredible! The enemy has a much larger army than we thought!"

Fu Chien's shock and loss of confidence communicated itself quickly to those under his command and resulted in great confusion.

This led to a defeat that he could not have imagined. In the end, the Eastern Tsin's tactical illusion, in which they created more from less, had caused Fu Chien to make something of nothing, and his misjudgment brought about his own downfall.

CROSS OVER TO CH'EN TS'ANG IN THE DARK

暗渡陳倉

示之以動、
利其静而有主。
益動而巽。

By displaying something,
there will be motion.
Take advantage of this basic stillness and
place your foundation in it.
Increase moves and then follow through.[1]

This is a strategy in which you utilize a series of
maneuvers. Develop a feint operation, and if the
enemy is taken in by your activity and strengthens
his defense at the focus of your feint, then secretly
marshal your forces and commence a surprise attack
from a different direction.

"Cross Over to Ch'en Ts'ang in the Dark" is a strategy in which you pretend to strike point A, but in fact strike point B. In conception, it is similar to Strategy 6, "Be Heard in the East, Strike in the West." Needless to say, the real object is point B. You hide that aim, first striking point A and drawing the enemy's attention there. Having done this, you now strike at point B. Because you can strike at the point of the enemy's inattentiveness and weakness, your chance of victory is extremely high.

The success or failure of this strategy, however, depends entirely on the success or failure of the feint tactic. In order to make your feint tactic a success, you must proceed carefully with the preparation for the maneuver to draw the enemy in.

If this is not accomplished, the feint tactic will not be a success and your strategy will fail.

◉ Han Hsin Outflanks His Opponent

This strategy took its present form from the saying, "Construct the plank road in the light of day, cross over to Ch'en Ts'ang in the dark," and is based on a tactic of the Han-period general Han Hsin.

After the destruction of the Ch'in dynasty, Hsiang Yu awarded Liu Pang the position of ruler of Han. Liu Pang took up his post and stationed troops throughout Han. In traveling from the Land within the Passes [Shensi] to Han, Liu Pang had to cross over the Ch'in Ling mountain range and traverse a road that bore through the mountains and continued over a precipice via a suspension bridge. This was called the Plank Road of Shu. On his way to occupying the state of Han, Liu Pang passed over the Plank Road and reduced it to ashes.

This deed was done to indicate that he had no intention of returning to the Land within the Passes and thus to assuage the vigilance of Hsiang Yu and underscore that in his new, more powerful position he, Liu Pang, posed no threat. Hsiang Yu acknowledged this action, entrusted the rule of the Land within the Passes to other generals, and then withdrew to his own home base in the east.

After a year Liu Pang decided to challenge Hsiang Yu's hegemony and, entrusting Han Hsin to the position of commanding general, he once again set out to strike at the Land within the Passes.

At this point, Han Hsin sent laborers out to deal with the reconstruction of the Plank Road. Signaling that he would take up a strong offensive position to strike after crossing the bridge, he drew the enemy's attention to the reconstruction of the Plank Road. The enemy responded by strengthening its defenses in that area. Meanwhile, Han Hsin secretly advanced his army along an ancient, roundabout road and defeated the enemy garrison at Ch'en Ts'ang, a decisive victory that ensured he had the Land within the Passes in the palm of his hand.

⊛ Chiang Wei's Unconvincing Strategy

As mentioned previously, the success or failure of this strategy relies on the strength of the feint tactic. If the feint fails to convince the enemy, or their leaders simply see through it, then all will come to naught.

During the period of the Three Kingdoms, the eccentric Shu general Chiang Wei led his army to invade the state of Wei. The man who went to meet the attack was the Wei governor general of Nan-an, Teng Ai.

Teng Ai successfully stopped the Shu army, but he noted that "the enemy has not retreated far, so there is a possibility that he will attack again. We must stay here and strengthen our guard."

So saying, he bivouacked on the northern bank of the Pai River and kept an eye on the enemy's moves. On the fourth day, Chiang Wei dispatched a subordinate, Liao Hua, to the southern bank of the Pai River and had him take up a position of attack with army troops.

Teng Ai observed the proceedings but was unconvinced of the

sincerity of the maneuver. He gathered his subordinate generals together and said, "Chiang Wei's army doubled back quite abruptly to the south bank. Our own forces are inferior to his, so it's natural that he should cross the river and attack. And yet from what we can see, there is no indication of his doing so. It seems to me that Liao Hua's role is to tie us down here and distract us, while Chiang Wei himself leads an army to invade our fortress at T'ao."

That night, Teng Ai gathered his troops, went directly to the fortress at T'ao along a secret path, and strengthened its defenses. As Teng Ai had suspected, Chiang Wei crossed the T'ao River and advanced to attack, but as Teng Ai had already strengthened his defenses, nothing was gained and Chiang Wei was forced to withdraw.

Chiang Wei employed the strategy of "Cross Over to Ch'en Ts'ang in the Dark," but his opponent Teng Ai saw through his plot, and Chiang Wei's strategy ultimately backfired.

◉ The Strategy behind the Landing at Normandy

Many readers might be surprised to learn that "Cross Over to Ch'en Ts'ang in the Dark" was used successfully by the Allies in one of the landmark battles toward the end of World War II—the landing at Normandy.

Looking at the map, it is clear that in crossing the channel from the southeast part of England to the coast of France, landing in the province of Pas de Calais—rather than Normandy—is the closest in terms of distance and provides the best conditions for both the transport of material and air support. In short, it was the obvious and most advantageous choice for the Allies. The German army judged this the most suitable location for a counteroffensive to begin and watched it carefully. The Allies spread false information through agents and double agents that indeed Pas de Calais was their objective. They sent out incessant information confirming the plan and flew concentrated bombing sorties over the area, giving the impression that the landing would be nearby. The Germans prepared for an attack by building up a huge defensive position there.

With the German army's attention focused on Pas de Calais, the Allies began their invasion at Normandy and were able to succeed due to their feint operation and meticulous preparation.

ON THE DISTANT SHORE, WATCH FOR FIRE

隔岸観火

陽乖序乱、陰以待逆。
暴戻恣睢、其勢自斃。
順以動予、予順以動。

*When discord is apparent and heralds chaos,
wait in the shadows for dissent from within.
Violent obstinacy and selfish action will of
its own force self-destruct.
"With order, motion is enthusiastic.
Enthusiasm with order moves."*[1]

If the enemy's internal contradictions deepen, and their internal regulations fall apart, watch steadily and quietly, and wait for an eruption of something irregular. From enmity and antagonism, their killing of each other begins—their inevitable demise winding along the road of self-destruction. You, however, should assume a position of looking on with folded arms. Good fortune waits and sleeps.

"On the Distant Shore, Watch for Fire" assumes an attitude of watching and waiting. The following is found in *The Art of War*:

> Wise rulers and generals always strive to attain their purpose in war with an attitude of caution. If they do not have favorable conditions and an invincible force, they do not commence with strategies and mobilizations; and unless absolutely unavoidable, they do not embark on any military activities at all.

Even if your military force is superior, to set out on an attack blindly is unwise. And, even if you win a temporary victory, your side will be unable to avoid considerable bloodshed. So even if you consider this a victory, you cannot say that it is a laudable way of winning; it is nothing more than a Pyrrhic victory.

When there is evidence of internal discord within your opponent's ranks, it is advisable to watch steadily and quietly and to wait for your opponent's self-destruction. To take advantage of the situation and attack when your opponents are beginning to suffer internal discord is one method, but doing so may, contrary to what you desire, serve to unite them. Thus attacking when you notice the first strains of discord cannot be called an expedient plan. At such a time, you should assume a watchful attitude and wait for your opponents to self-destruct. This is the strategy known as "On the Distant Shore, Watch for Fire."

A corollary tactic is summed up in the phrase, "A fisherman's benefit."[2] This strategy involves creating a situation that encourages your opponents to fight each other, thus dissipating their own forces, while you yourself preserve your strength and wait for your opponents to destroy themselves from within. Putting this second tactic to work is easiest when you notice internal dissention. Both strategies conform with Sun Tzu's tenet of "winning without fighting."

⊛ Attack versus Watchful Patience—Strategy 5 Versus Strategy 9

The internal strife or contradictions of an opponent provide a chance for you to take advantage of him. To attack your opponent without hesitation and defeat him utterly is the fifth strategy, "Take Advantage of the Fire to Plunder the Goods." The ninth strategy, "On the Distant Shore, Watch for Fire," also has the opponent's internal strife and contradictions as prerequisites. However, this ploy involves waiting for your opponent's internal collapse to the very end. From the point of aiming for a situation of "A wet hand easily grabs bubbles,"[3] this may be far and away more cunning than the fifth strategy.

Even if an opponent makes no attempt to hide his internal discord from you, there is a possibility that an unskillful demonstration of aggression may only serve to unify him. Watch steadily and quietly and wait for his internal collapse, by far the wiser of the two policies.

Deciding which strategy to use demands careful consideration: it is difficult to judge whether one should strike forcefully or simply watch quietly. There are many cases of leaders waiting patiently on the sidelines for signs of internal strife in the enemy's ranks, only to see their chance for attack evaporate before their eyes. If you do decide to attack, strike as swiftly as lightning, move as quickly as a spark flying off a stone.

In either case, penetrating vision is essential. When you watch quietly, you must do so thoroughly.

⊛ Ts'ao Ts'ao's "On the Distant Shore, Watch for Fire"

In *The Romance of the Three Kingdoms*, Ts'ao Ts'ao defeated Yuan Shao at the Battle of Kuan Tu and gained control over all of northern China. Yuan Shao's sons, Yuan Shang and Yuan Hsi, escaped, making their way to safety among the Wu-wan, a non-Chinese people in north China, with the intention of resisting Ts'ao Ts'ao. To eliminate the threat in the north, it would be necessary for Ts'ao Ts'ao to strike the Wu-wan.

Therefore, in the year 207 of the Western calendar, Ts'ao Ts'ao set forth to subjugate the Wu-wan, and annihilated them with little effort. Yuan Shang and Yuan Hsi fled and took refuge with Sun K'ang, the duke of Liao Tung. Previously, the duke had successfully defended himself in Liao Tung against Ts'ao Ts'ao. With a common enemy, the Yuan brothers felt assured of a safe haven. Furthermore, they secretly reasoned that if the chance presented itself, they would usurp Sun K'ang's position, entrench themselves at Liao Tung, and from their new base resist Ts'ao Ts'ao.

At this point, the officers of Ts'ao Ts'ao's staff recommended immediately advancing their army to Liao Tung, subjugating Duke Sun K'ang, and at the same time annihilating Yuan Shang and his brother.

But Ts'ao Ts'ao vehemently refused, saying, "No, no. I'm thinking that Yuan Shang and Yuan Hsi will be finished off by Sun K'ang. We needn't take the trouble of mobilizing the army now."

So saying, he withdrew to his capital. Sure enough, the words were barely out of his mouth when the heads of Yuan Shang and Yuan Hsi were delivered to him from Sun K'ang.

The staff officers could not understand why this had happened. When they inquired about the apparent betrayal, Ts'ao Ts'ao replied, "The duke feared the influence of Yuan Shang and his followers from the very beginning. If I had mobilized my army and attacked, I suppose they would have combined forces against us, but by leaving them alone, it was only a matter of time before they began fighting among themselves. This is just the natural course of events."

It is in situations like this, when internal conflict is probable, that "On the Distant Shore, Watch for Fire" should be applied.

Strategy **10**

Conceal a Sword Behind a Smile

笑裏蔵刀

信而安之、陰以図之。
備而後動、勿使有変。
剛中柔外也。

With an easy manner,
put your enemy at ease.
In obscurity, make your plans.
Make preparations, then move.
Do not let your plans change.
This is being strong within and soft without.

Demonstrate a friendly sincerity and dissolve the enemy's sense of vigilance; secretly devise a strategy to knock him down. Only act after you have fully arranged your preparations. Moreover, at that time, you must hide your true intentions until the very last moment. This is a strategy in which you conceal a dagger in your breast, while on the surface you conduct yourself with a smile.

"Conceal a Sword behind a Smile" is, as the words imply, a tactic of approaching your opponent with a friendly demeanor, then attacking with a single blow when he drops his vigilance. Needless to say, remaining cheerful to the very end is a prerequisite to softening his defenses. The chances of your success rise according to the degree that you can truly accomplish this strategy. On the other hand, if you suspect that you are on the receiving end of this strategy, you must quickly confirm the fact and devise a counterstrategy. If you neglect to follow up with a defense, you will fall helplessly into the enemy's trap.

Sun Tzu said:

> While the enemy's messenger humbly offers a truce, the enemy himself will be steadily strengthening his defenses and in fact will be preparing plans for an attack . . . When words of peace suddenly appear in the opposing camp, there will be some sort of strategy afloat.

In short, when the enemy approaches with endearing words, you must be suspicious and assume he is hiding some other aim.

The Emperor's Humiliating Lesson

On the eve of the First Emperor's unification of China in the final days of the Warring States period, an incident occurred that taught the emperor a hard and humbling lesson.

Ching K'o received a secret order from Prince Tan of the state of Yen and, writing the following poem acknowledging his resolve and preparedness for death, made his way to the capital of Ch'in:

> The wind blows lonely, lonely,
> The waters of the Yi River run cold.
> Once the brave soldiers depart,
> They do not come home again.

Prince Tan had ordered his retainer to assassinate the emperor, a task that, whether successfully carried out or not, meant Ching K'o would never see Yen again. When Ching K'o set out, he brought with him two gifts to sway the First Emperor. One was the head of General Fan Yu-chih, who had fled from Ch'in to Yen and was considered by the First Emperor to be a traitor. Ching K'o had carefully weighed Fan's standing and then convinced the exiled general that by committing suicide and allowing his head to be delivered to the emperor as a gift, the emperor could be brought down. The general complied.

The second gift was a map of Tu-k'ang, the most fertile region in Yen. Presenting this map to the emperor signaled Prince Tan's intention of giving Tu-k'ang to the emperor as tribute.

But as attractive as these gifts were, they did not secure Ching K'o an audience with the First Emperor. Next, Ching K'o offered a gift of over a thousand pieces of gold to Meng-chia, the First Emperor's favorite retainer, and asked him to intercede. The lure of a thousand pieces of gold soon ensnared the retainer.

Meng-chia went to the First Emperor and said, "The ruler of Yen fully respects your highness's authority and has ended resistance to your rule. All of his nobles are at your service and one of them has brought an exceedingly generous tribute. He has hesitated to come and speak these words to you himself but has, out of great respect to your highness, cut off the head of Fan Yu-chih and sent it along with a map of Tu-k'ang to be presented to you by his messenger. What do you think? Shall I take care of this?"

This appeared to persuade the First Emperor, and he let his guard down.

Granted an audience, Ching K'o met the emperor and pulled a hidden dagger. The emperor was swift and dodged the blow. Ching K'o was restrained and promptly executed. The emperor had survived the attempt on his life but had learned a humiliating lesson in the art of "Conceal a Sword behind a Smile."

⚙ A Humble Retainer Outwits a More Experienced Leader

During the period of the Three Kingdoms, Kuan Yu of Shu was responsible for the province of Ching and, while occupying Chiang-ling, mobilized and advanced toward the north, surrounding the fortress at Fan in the territory of Wei.

At the time, the man responsible for the state of Wu, a wise general by the name of Lu Meng, was stationed at Lu-k'ou and carefully watched Kuan Yu's moves. With Kuan Yu's army marching north, Chiang-ling was more vulnerable than before. But Kuan Yu kept a close watch on Lu Meng as well, and indeed it would have been foolish of him to overlook Lu Meng's proximity. Leaving a respectable military force in Chiang-ling, Kuan Yu guarded himself against any move Lu Meng might make.

Thus, in order to seize Chiang-ling, Lu Meng would first have to disarm Kuan Yu's suspicions. Lu Meng pleaded illness and withdrew to his capital, appointing an unknown commissioned officer by the name of Lu Sun to oversee Lu-k'ou. Lu Sun[1] was an untested leader. When Kuan Yu heard that a youngster like Lu Sun had been appointed in place of the experienced Lu Meng, he was overjoyed.

However, although Lu Sun was young in years, he was the possessor of extraordinary artifice. As soon as he proceeded to Lu-k'ou, he immediately sent a letter to Kuan Yu, praising him as a man of valor and professing his own humble inability. This was an effort to assume a humble attitude in order to slacken Kuan Yu's vigilance.

Convinced by this communiqué of the ineffectiveness of the new appointee, Kuan Yu dropped his guard and withdrew the entire force that had been posted at Chiang-ling, and threw them into his ambitious attack of the fortress at Fan. Lu Meng seized the moment and secretly led his army to Chiang-ling, capturing it without a fight.

Having fallen for the "Conceal a Sword Behind a Smile" strategy, the humiliated Kuan Yu tragically committed suicide.

⊛ The Two-faced Character of "Conceal a Sword behind a Smile"

During the T'ang dynasty there was a man by the name of Li I-fu. To look at him, he would seem to have a gentle character. When talking to people, he never stopped smiling. However, as soon as he was appointed councilor and began to wield authority, anyone who disagreed with him in the least was put down mercilessly. The people of that time thus feared him and would often say, "I-fu has a sword in his smile." This phrase meant that a person was hiding trickery behind a "smiling face," and in Li I-fu's case, it was his fellow high officials in the government that were the objects of his strategy. In the end, however, he incurred their enmity and was overthrown.

Nevertheless, if the object of the "sword" that you employ is an enemy, the story is quite different.

During the Sung dynasty, the governor of the province of Wei, a man by the name of Ts'ao Wei, was keeping the activities of the Tangut (a non-Chinese people living in the west) in check. He commanded a strict military presence and was greatly feared by these people. One day, he gathered all the generals under his command and held a drinking party for them. Suddenly, a report came in that several thousand of his soldiers had risen in revolt and deserted to the Tangut. The generals all looked at each other in dismay, but Ts'ao Wei alone chatted on, unruffled by the news. Nonchalantly he said, "They're only acting under my orders. Calm down."

When this was repeated to the Tangut, they felt certain that they had fallen into a trap set by the Sung soldiers that had defected to them, and in order to eliminate the perceived threat killed them all.

When a man is hard-pressed, if he is able to remain totally unperturbed and carry off the strategy of "Conceal a Sword behind a Smile," his ability as a leader cannot be questioned.

SACRIFICE THE PEACH TO SECURE THE PLUM

李代桃僵

勢必有損、損陰以益陽。

Force absolutely incurs damage.
By decreasing yin, one increases yang.

Depending on how the tide of war develops, there
will be situations in which you must be resolved to
suffer damage. In such cases, you must secure a
general victory in exchange for limited damage.

"Sacrifice the Peach to Secure the Plum" is a strategy in which you sacrifice something of lesser value (the peach) to obtain an object or goal of greater value (the plum). The same idea is behind "Let him cut your skin while you cut his flesh; let him cut your flesh while you cut his bones."

This is a matter of battle, so you must be resolved to suffer some damage. At such a time, it is a given that one would seek to limit the amount of damage one sustains. At the same time, you must compensate by obtaining a benefit that exceeds the damage. In the games of *go* or chess, pieces are often sacrificed with the goal of grasping the greater victory.

⊛ Sun Pin's Technique for Absolute Victory

Sun Pin was invited to be a guest of the Ch'i general T'ien Chi, who at the time was addicted to gambling. The general enjoyed betting with the various dukes of Ch'i on chariot races. Sun Pin observed the races carefully and could see that, at the starting gate, the three pairs of chariots were divided into upper, middle, and lower classes; but within the same class, the competing horses were similar in strength.

After considerable thought, he approached T'ien Chi and said, "I can show you a foolproof way to win your next bet."

T'ien Chi got very excited and went around, not only to the dukes but to the ruler himself, and challenged them all to a great match with a thousand pieces of gold.

Accordingly, on the day of the race, Sun Pin whispered to T'ien Chi, "Take your slowest chariot and pair it up with the fastest of the other party's. Then, take your fastest horse and pair it against their second fastest. Then take your second fastest and pair it against their third fastest."

As a result, he suffered only one loss but gained two victories, and successfully put away a great deal of money.

This is a clever application of "Sacrifice the Peach to Secure the Plum" and typical of the strategy.

⊕ Battle of the Dnieper River

One of the greatest battles of World War II took place when the Soviets were attacked by the German army, and then opened up a general counteroffensive. In the middle of this counteroffensive, in the autumn of 1943, a battle was fought crossing the Dnieper River with the aim of recapturing Kiev.

At this time, two separate battalions from the 381st army division, which were the Soviet vanguard, split off from the main force, crossed the Dnieper from a point where they had broken through a northern section of Kiev, and established a beachhead. The German army launched a large number of tanks and began a ferocious counteroffensive. The Soviet military headquarters ordered a stubborn defense of the beachhead, the strategy of which was to draw in the German army.

As expected, the German army focused its attention on recapturing the beachhead and launched a large military force to dislodge the Soviets. In the opening that was thus created, the 381st division's main force turned to the south and easily succeeded in crossing the river. However, the two battalions that had been ordered to stubbornly defend the beachhead were attacked ferociously by the German troops and were almost entirely annihilated.

This is "killing the small to save the large." In real-life battle such inhuman decisions are often forcefully employed.

⊕ In Business and War, Sow Loss and Reap Gain

A leader lacking talent may be easily distracted by a limited loss. Both in war and in business, loss is something one wants to avoid. When loss is unavoidable, the question then becomes, in what way can the loss be linked to future gain? Do not become flustered in the face of loss, but seek to calmly discern what benefit can be drawn from it.

Sun Tzu said the following:

> The wise person will inevitably think of things from the two aspects of loss and gain. If he will do so, events will progress smoothly. Conversely, when one suffers a loss, he should consider it from the aspect of receiving some gain from that loss. If he will do this, he will easily bring the event to a conclusion without being troubled.

LEAD AWAY THE SHEEP WHEN CONDITIONS ARE RIGHT

順手牽羊

微隙在所必乘。

微利在所必得。

少陰、少陽。

Always take advantage of a minute opening;
always take a minute gain.
Small yin becomes small yang.

If you discover an opening, you must take advantage of it without delay, no matter how small an opening it may be. If there is benefit to be gained, you must take possession of it without hesitation, no matter how small that benefit may be. No matter how minor your enemy's ineptitude, if you are able to take advantage of it, that in itself approaches victory.

"Lead Away the Sheep When Conditions Are Right" originally meant to behave unscrupulously if circumstances put something within reach. However, when it concerns battle tactics and techniques, it is nothing more than a strategy of taking advantage of an enemy's opening and amplifying war results in a calculating way. The conditions that will realize this strategy are the following:

- The original goal must remain the foremost target.
- The tangential goal must be an easily obtained benefit that tumbles into one's lap.
- When reaching for the tangential goal, there must be no obstacle created to pursuing the original goal.

◉ The Calculating Methods of Overseas Chinese Merchants

Many Chinese merchants rush overseas without a penny in their pockets. Their capital is nothing more than their own bodies. They often start with just pennies, yet often accomplish great things. In Chinese, this phenomenon is summed up in the phrase "To raise a house with empty hands."

In such circumstances, there is no leisure for cutting as elegant a figure as you might like, and you must put your hand to anything, even those things that people find distasteful. A business that requires neither cutting an elegant figure nor capital, but which includes good remuneration into the bargain, is not something commonly encountered. If the profit of a single penny is to be gained, it is not uncommon for the overseas Chinese merchant to make it his own, without regard for how he looks.

In a book entitled *The Methods of the Overseas Chinese Merchant*, the following story is introduced:

A long time ago, an overseas Chinese watchman, past the age of thirty, sold beer to students in his spare time. The beer was incredibly inexpensive. When a customer asked if he had a direct connection to the top wholesaler since he sold the beer at such low prices, he responded, "No, I sell the beer at cost."

The Chinese merchant seemed to be hiding something. He took great care of the boxes that contained a dozen of the beer bottles, and he made his profit only on the boxes themselves, taking a small fee when a customer bought in quantity.

Do not consider the man foolish. This is a case of dust piling up until it finally becomes a mountain. The merchant may well have put away enough capital from his streamlined beer business to start a more profitable business.

⊛ A Leader's Capacity for Circumstantial Judgment

There are leaders who, once a goal is set, take no notice of anything else but only advance headlong toward that goal. While there is nothing inherently wrong with that strategy, it does appear dogmatic and stubborn.

When the tide of war progresses in an advantageous way, this unyielding method is fine. But if their position weakens, then such single-minded leaders lose the capacity for strategic leadership. Another type of leader is easily distracted by the smallest gains and loses sight of their original goal. Both courses are wrong.

The pursuit of the goal must be sustained, not diluted. At the same time, one must possess the flexibility to recognize conditions in which one can increase one's military achievements or capacity by absorbing smaller benefits along the way. In order to correctly weigh the options and the benefits, it is essential to be able to view emerging circumstances with a calm judgment.

Part **III**

STRATEGIES FOR ATTACK

In situations when a battle involves facing an opponent with superior numbers, you should avoid fighting him head on. There is not one single advantage in engaging in a futile war of attrition. At such times, you must actively employ some strategy and aim at some efficient way of victory.

"Beat the Grass, Surprise the Snake" has two meanings. The first is a strategy of sounding out the situation and inferring your opponent's moves. *The Art of War* says, "If you know the enemy and know yourself, you may fight a hundred battles without danger." It also continually stresses the importance of intelligence activity. But what you are able to ascertain by intelligence activity is in itself limited, and it is difficult to obtain intelligence concerning the detailed disposition of units. Thus, what becomes essential is understanding your opponent's movements as they relate to his strategic activities. For such, you must first sound out the situation with reconnaissance activities, and then watch your opponent's response.

Secondly, you beat the grass in order to more fully understand the snake's circumstance; you do not beat the snake. This tactic includes the idea of smoking out information. In other words, you gradually establish evidence from smaller elements in your environment in order to grasp something large.

Regardless of the approach, however, this strategy targets the surrounding grass to take the measure of the snake's tendencies and movements.

⊛ England's Strategy in the Suez War

In 1956, the Suez War erupted, a conflict involving Egypt, England, France, and Israel. Egypt boldly announced that it was nationalizing the Suez Canal. England and France then embarked on an action of armed intervention and landed airborne troops on the portside of the canal's entryway.

While this maneuver appeared to be an attack, in reality it was nothing more than a staged puppet show of men and guns, motivated, of course, by the need to uncover the strength of Egypt's defense. Not perceiving this for the ploy that it was, the Egyptian army rained a concentrated bombardment on the puppets, exposing the strengths and weaknesses of their military.

With this new information, English and French forces grasped the placement of their opponent's firepower and troops and immediately attacked the Egyptian defensive positions, destroying them entirely. After that, they were able to deploy an effective strategy of landing and disembarkation.

⊛ Sound Out the Situation and Watch the Reaction

"Beat the Grass and Surprise the Snake" is an efficacious weapon when negotiation and persuasion is the order of the day. In such situations, it is not desirable for you to rattle off unilaterally everything you have to offer or want to say all in one go. In order to negotiate effectively and achieve your end, you must first understand your opponent's true intentions and the means he has at hand. To that end you can employ this strategy to sound him out and gather information based on his response. Once you have gathered your information, you then formulate your own counterstrategy.

Borrow the Corpse, Revive Its Soul

借屍還魂

有用者、不可借。
不能用者、求借。
借不能用者而用之、
匪我求童蒙、童蒙求我。

You should not hire someone who is useful.
You should seek a person
who is incompetent and useless.
Hire the incompetent and useless, and use him.
Do not seek a foolish youth,
for he will seek you out.[1]

For this strategy, the independent person will be difficult to manage and impossible to put to use. However, the person who exists by relying on the strength of others will seek your assistance. Take advantage of such a person and seize your opportunity. This is nothing more than a strategy to manage your opponent, rather than letting him control you.

"Borrow the Corpse, Revive Its Soul" is the important strategy of using those you can take advantage of to increase your own power. Of course, there is more than one way to take advantage of people or situations. Here are three examples:

- You use them as a breakwater for your own self-defense.
- You use them as a cloak of invisibility as you increase your own power.
- You use them as steppingstones for enlarging of your own foothold.

Moreover, as a prerequisite for taking advantage of someone, it is essential that the other person's power be weak but still worth using. If the other person's power is insubstantial and not worth exploiting, discard him outright.

◉ Even a Shepherd is Worth Taking Advantage of

As soon as the First Emperor of Ch'in died, rebellions broke out all over China in resistance to Ch'in's oppression. Those who spearheaded these rebellions were men from the farming class, such as Ch'en Sheng and Wu K'uang; but Hsiang Liang and Hsiang Yu of Ch'u and Liang Pang from P'ei also promptly joined the uprisings.

After Ch'en Sheng and Wu K'uang were killed in the revolts against the Ch'in, the formation of the anti-Ch'in alliance continued under the drumbeat of Hsiang Liang. At that time, the strategist Fan Tseng spoke the following words to Hsiang Liang:

"It is natural that Ch'en Sheng was defeated. This is because among the six states that brought down the Ch'in, those who resented the Ch'in the most were the people of Ch'u. Ch'en Sheng, however, did not understand this fact and, while he took the lead and raised an army, he ignored the descendants of the ruler of Ch'u, and became king himself. Thus it is not unreasonable that his struggle ended with his losing his life. On the other hand, when you raised an army in Chiang Tung, the generals who sprang to their feet everywhere in Ch'u hurried to join you. This is because—along with your being from a family of military leaders for the Ch'u for generations—they expect you to restore the royal house. I hope you will not forget this fact."

Hsiang Liang saw the foresight behind Fan Tseng's words. He quickly sought out a descendant of the former king of Ch'u—a man by the name of Hsien, who was now employed as a shepherd—and established him as the successor of the former ruler, giving him the name Huai. Eventually, this man became the nominal leader of the anti-Ch'in alliance.

The armies of the alliance rallied around the name of King Huai and advanced to attack the Ch'in capital at Hsien-yang. However, once the Ch'in were defeated, King Huai's usefulness had been spent and he was finally disposed of at the hand of Hsiang Yu, who had risen to become the most powerful man of the alliance armies.

⊛ How Ts'ao Ts'ao Took Advantage of the Emperor

During the chaotic period of *The Romance of the Three Kingdoms*, Ts'ao Ts'ao raised an army, gathering it together from a military force of just a few thousand soldiers. After a number of years, he built up an independent power base in the province of Yen, located in the basin of the Yellow River. However, his power was still not great enough to supplant that of his rivals. In order to further increase his base, he played several strategic cards to prepare for the future. One of these cards was receiving the current emperor at Ts'ao Ts'ao's own home base in Hsu.

Emperor Hsien, who was the last emperor at the court of the Later Han, was struggling with his own ravaged capital, at times facing starvation. Ts'ao Ts'ao's rivals, who had held their ground in their various states, had opened up their own punitive expeditions. Not one of them would extend a hand to help the emperor.

To Ts'ao Ts'ao, the significance of the emperor's visit was invaluable. Even though his authority had waned, the emperor was still the emperor. Whether in moving troops or issuing orders to rivals, there was a great difference in political capital if the emperor headed one's forces. Thus, from a political standpoint, once Ts'ao Ts'ao decided to support the emperor he rose a head above the other chieftains.

Ts'ao Ts'ao manipulated Emperor Hsien like a puppet, taking advantage of the man's authority while increasing his own strength. In doing so, he became the most powerful man of the period. Yet he did not seek to raise himself above the emperor in name. Instead, he held the power and let the emperor keep his throne.

◉ Liu Pei Takes Shu

Liu Pei, one of Ts'ao Ts'ao's rivals, also found himself suddenly thrust into a position where he could profit by employing the strategy of "Borrow the Corpse, Revive Its Soul."

Liu Pei had been eager to accomplish something in Shu, but a man by the name of Liu Chang had previously established himself there and governed the region skillfully and without incurring the anger of any rivals. Thus, Liu Pei had no real pretext with which to mobilize an army. Liu Chang, however, felt some unease about the defense of Shu's north, and he sought Liu Pei's help on the basis of their shared family name.

Liu Pei, spotting an opportunity, thought, "Any boat to get across the river" and, leading an army, headed out for Shu. Profiting from some pretense, he then attacked Liu Chang and, in the end, took possession of Shu.

Beckoned as an ally, he found fault with the other party and took over what he saw as the "corpse" of Liu Chang to pave his rise to power.

PACIFY THE TIGER THEN LEAD IT FROM THE MOUNTAIN

調虎離山

待天以因之、用人以誘之。
往蹇来返。

Wait for Heaven, and thus bring distress.
Employ someone else, and thus entice.
Going out, there is obstruction;
remaining home, there is return.[1]

When blessed with beneficial natural conditions,
take advantage of them to antagonize the enemy;
further, entice him by scattering bait he is liable to
take. When danger can be forecast, even though
you make the attack, deliberately show your opponent an opening you wish him to strike.

The "tiger" of this strategy means a formidable enemy; the "mountain" means his stronghold. The tiger that lives in a mountain blessed by advantageous natural conditions is difficult to defeat. The idea is that, in order to subdue a well-entrenched tiger, you must first lure him from the mountain. Speaking from the point of battle strategies and tactics, this strategy includes the following two methods:

- When the enemy is entrenched in a staunchly defended castle or stronghold, this strategy requires the abandonment of the fortress.
- In the case of direct confrontation, take the direction of the enemy's attack to another place and mitigate the pressure at the front.

In either case, to make a success of this strategy, it is essential to devise a trick to lure the enemy out. The skill with which this trick is conceived and carried out is the key.

⊕ Yu Hsu Lures the Tiger

Toward the end of the period of the court of the Later Han, a tribe of non-Chinese people in western China called the Ch'iang rose in rebellion and invaded Wu Tu. After the invasion, a man by the name of Yu Hsu was appointed the governor of Wu Tu and ordered to subjugate the tribe. Leading his troops to take up this new appointment, Yu Hsu's procession was blocked by an army of the Ch'iang as it approached Chen Ts'ang, and it was unable to advance any further.

After some thought, Yu Hsu sent out an official notice requesting reinforcements from the imperial court, stating that he would await their arrival before moving forward. The Ch'iang tribe heard of Yu Hsu's decision and judged that his army would remain stationary for the near future. With this information in hand, the Ch'iang tribe decided to take advantage of Yu Hsu's misfortune. They divided their troops, then attacked the neighboring provinces, going on to pillage property and goods.

As soon as Yu Hsu confirmed that the Ch'iang had split their forces, he marched swiftly along the road day and night toward the fortress at Wu Tu.

Furthermore, each time his army stopped to rest, he ordered the soldiers to build and light more disposable clay cooking ovens, and to multiply the number of ovens every day. When the remaining Ch'iang forces saw the number of ovens, they were certain that the reinforcements had arrived and did not dare attack. In this way, Yu Hsu broke through the blockade, entered the fortress at Wu Tu, and having an overwhelming advantage now that the Ch'iang forces were divided, was able to destroy the Ch'iang army.

Yu Hsu's false message to the imperial court drew the tiger of Ch'iang from the mountain.

⊛ Han Hsin Encamps with His Back to a Stream

This event occurred when Han Hsin of the Han dynasty attacked Chao. The troops that Han Hsin led numbered less than ten thousand, while his opponents' ran to two hundred thousand and were, moreover, entrenched in a secure and firm fortress.

Clearly, he had no chance of victory with a direct attack, so Han Hsin devised a plan to change the odds. First, he selected two thousand soldiers, supplied each with a red Han flag, and ordered them to prepare to hide in a recess of the mountain that looked down upon the Chao army's fortress.

He then revealed his plan:

"In tomorrow's battle, the main force will attack and then pretend to retreat. We will set up camp so they think us foolish. Seeing our foolishness, the enemy will leave his fortress and chase us down in hopes of finishing us off. They will believe us easy prey. Once they leave the fort, the two thousand will rush into the fortress from their hiding place in the mountains, take down the white flags of the Chao, and hoist all two thousand red flags."

With that, Han Hsin ordered the remainder of the main troops to mobilize and then to encamp with their backs to the river that flowed in front of Chao's army.

When morning came, the Chao army took note of the situation and laughed scornfully, deriding Han Hsin as a fool who knew nothing about the military arts. Surely, no matter which military books one studies, from *The Art of War* on down, it was nowhere written that you should encamp with your back to a river and cut off your route of escape.

According to plan, after the enemy had seen his encampment, Han Hsin led a battalion and attacked the fortress. The Chao army now regarded their opponents with such disdain that without further thought they left the fortress in a counterattack. Han Hsin abandoned his insignias, immediately retreated, and fled to the encampment along the banks of the river, drawing the Chao army further and further from the fortress.

Inevitably his army ran up against the river, and with no place to flee, they turned to fight. Every one of Han Hsin's troops fought desperately, and the Chao army—which despite being so superior in numbers—had more than they could deal with.

Meanwhile, the detached force that had hidden in the mountain entered and occupied the abandoned fortress. Seeing the fortress "captured" and so many enemy flags waving, the Chao troops' morale began to waver. Next, Han Hsin's troops attacked from the rear. This maneuver proved to be deadly, and it utterly destroyed the spirits of the Chao troops, who were annihilated without mercy.

With his "last stand,"[2] Han Hsin drew out his troops' best efforts and lured out his opponents with the strategy of "Pacify the Tiger Then Lead It from the Mountain."

IF YOU COVET IT, LEAVE IT ALONE

欲擒姑縱

逼則反兵。　走則減勢。
緊隨勿迫。　累其気力、
消其闘志、　散而後擒、
兵不血刃。　需、有孚、光。

Press them severely and enemy soldiers
will turn on you.
Let them run, and their power will decrease.
Do not press them too hard. Let their vigor
tire; let their will to fight extinguish itself.
If you take the enemy after his forces scatter,
your soldiers will have no blood on their blades.
In waiting[1] is sincerity and light.

If you attack, cutting off the road of retreat, your
opponent will counterattack in desperation. If you
let your opponent retreat, his energy will naturally
dissipate. In your pursuit, you must not corner
him or press him too closely. If you wait to appre-
hend him until after his physical strength weakens, his will to fight will wane. The victory will be
yours without bloodshed. If you wait for the right
moment, you can expect a good result.

"If You Covet It, Leave It Alone" advocates allowing the enemy an avenue of escape. If you surround him completely and then press in on him, he may resolve to make a last stand and launch a furious counterattack, as in the saying, "A cornered rat will bite a cat." Pitted against an opponent fueled by desperation, there is the possibility that your own forces will suffer considerable damage as well. To avoid such a situation, you should not attack impetuously and should always allow an escape route for your enemy to retreat. Leaving open the option of escape is at the heart of this strategy.

In *The Art of War* there is the phrase, "Wu and Yueh in the same boat." The people of Wu and the people of Yueh had not gotten along for many years. Nevertheless, when riding together in a boat that is in imminent danger, they will unite and cooperate to save themselves despite their longstanding enmity. When an army finds itself cornered, a good leader will use the opportunity to rally the soldiers to fight with all their might. Such philosophy is expounded in *The Art of War*.

This strategy contends that forcing the enemy into such a corner must be avoided at all costs. In attacking a weaker enemy furiously without allowing him a route to retreat—which is an admission of defeat—you put him in a situation of "Wu and Yueh in the same boat," and suddenly there is the possibility of a spirited counterattack that could turn the tide of the battle against you. Therefore, Sun Tzu spoke of "not pressing a cornered enemy," warning against the foolishness of precipitous attacks.

⊛ Seven Releases, Seven Captures

In *The Romance of the Three Kingdoms*, when Chu Ko K'ung-ming pacified the rebellion of the non-Chinese people in the south, he used this tactic as a political strategy. The leader of the rebellion was a man by the name of Meng Huo, and when K'ung-ming was about to advance his army south, he notified all of his troops that they were not to kill Meng Huo, but to take him alive.

After a violent battle, Meng Huo was captured and brought before K'ung-ming. K'ung-ming gave him a tour of his troops, revealing his strength and position. "What do you think?" he asked.

"I suffered a defeat because I didn't understand your battle array before now," Meng Huo replied. "But now that you've been kind enough to show it to me, I'll beat you for sure the next time we fight."

K'ung-ming laughed and said, "That's interesting. Good enough, let this fellow go."

In this way, Meng Huo was seven times captured and seven times released (and thus was born the phrase, "Seven releases, seven captures").

The seventh time he was caught, even the intrepid Meng Huo must have felt at the bottom of his heart that he'd lost. When K'ung-ming once again was about to loosen his bonds and forgive him, Meng Huo said, "Your lordship is truly like a god. I will not turn against you again," and it is said that he never again left the man's side.

K'ung-ming complemented his military subjugation with the skill-ful political strategy of "If You Covet It, Leave It Alone," and in the end completely captured the hearts of the southern tribes.

⊛ A Cornered Rat Bites the Cat

During the reign of King Mang of Hsin, there were insurrections of outraged farmers' armies in every district, and one of those armies was led by K'un Yang. King Mang put Wang I in charge of an army of one hundred thousand men and ordered him to subjugate K'un Yang's army. Wang I completely surrounded a rebel fortress and made plans to attack. Thereupon his lieutenant-general, Yen Yu, advanced and advocated the following:

"Although K'un Yang has a small fortress, it has a stout defense and we cannot easily attack it and bring it down. Right now the main strength of the rebels is holed up in Yuan. If we first settle the situation in Yuan, I suspect that K'un Yang's rebels will scatter like the wind and show us their heels."

But Wang I did not heed this advice; he instead strengthened the encirclement of the fortress and made a reckless attack. The army of farmers in the fortress all begged to surrender, but Wang I would not listen.

At this point, Yen Yu again came forward and spoke: "In the military arts it is said that 'If you surround your enemy, you should always leave him a way of retreat.' Would it not be wise to let some of the rebels escape, and thus let them inform the others of our strength?"

But yet again, Wang I ignored his lieutenant-general.

Since the farmers' army in the fortress had not been allowed to surrender, and every way of escape had been closed off, there was nothing left for them but to make a desperate last stand. While they held their ground in this fashion, rebel reinforcements finally arrived. Suddenly Wang I's troops found themselves attacked from both inside and outside the fortress, and they were annihilated without mercy.

The cause of Wang I's destruction rests with his ignoring Yen Yu's suggested application of "If You Covet It, Leave It Alone." In attacking his opponent without providing a loophole for him to escape, Wang I opened the door to his own defeat, inadvertently demonstrating the axiom that "a cornered rat will bite a cat."

◉ Do Not Drive Your Opponent into a Corner—Further Examples

"If You Covet It, Leave It Alone" can also be instructive in the support of harmonious human relations. The *T'sai Ken Tan*,[2] a book that advocates a more humanistic approach to life, discusses this fact from various angles:

Human failings must be glossed over as much as possible. To

blindly expose another is to act in a blameworthy way yourself, and will come to no good end.

Even if you oust a bad man, you should leave him a way of retreat. If you torment him all the way to his shelter, he will feel like a rat trapped in a blocked hole with the path of retreat cut off. He will then have to fasten his teeth on something of consequence.

When you employ a person, there may be times when you are unable to handle the situation. At such a time, it is best to let it go for a little while and wait for the other person to change of his own accord. It is not good to busily interfere and make him intractable.

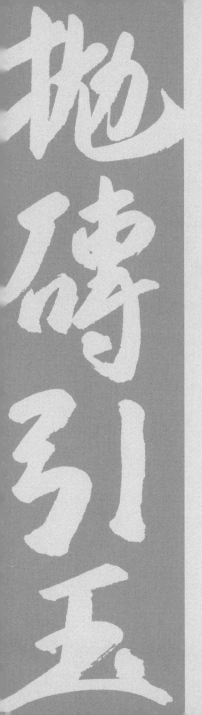

CAST A BRICK,
PULL IN JADE

拋磚引玉

類以誘之、擊蒙也。

Lure him with shams; strike the foolish youth.[1]

Use the misleading and muddle the enemy's judgment; throw his thoughts into chaos

The strategy "Cast a Brick, Pull in Jade" is expressed in Japanese with the phrase, "Fish for a sea bream with a shrimp." In other words, the idea is to scatter bait to attract the enemy, then annihilate him when he arrives. In this case, the more seemingly delicious the bait, the more efficacious the strategy will be. However, the bait must be disguised, otherwise the enemy will not bite. Therefore, a contrivance is necessary to mask the true purpose of the bait. In short, the point of this strategy is to create a contrivance that will lure and capture the enemy.

⊚ Luring the Enemy with a Decoy

This is an event that occurred during the Spring and Autumn period, when the state of Ch'u attacked the small state of Chiao. The armies of the Ch'u made their camp on the south face of Chiao's castle, and the general Ch'u Hsia approached the ruler of Ch'u and said:

"Chiao is a small state, and what's more, they lack discretion. Why don't we send some firewood porters into the mountains without a guard and lure the enemy out?"

In those days, firewood was a military necessity. Without firewood, the soldiers could not cook their food and would not be able to eat. By sending out porters to collect wood, the Ch'u were alerting the enemy to a supposed weakness. In truth, the Ch'u army already had sufficient supplies of wood, so the firewood porters were in fact acting as bait.

The ruler of Ch'u put this suggestion into operation. A group of thirty porters were sent into the mountains without a guard. The Chiao saw this as an opportunity and sent out a company of soldiers and captured the enemy's wood gatherers. The next day, the Ch'u army once again sent out unarmed porters into the mountains for wood. The Chiao, thinking the enemy was suffering a shortage of hot meals and hoping to prolong their anguish, once again sent out a large company of soldiers to chase down the porters.

Meanwhile, the Ch'u army, taking advantage of the overconfident Chiao, were lying in ambush near the northern gate of the fortress. When the gates were opened to snap up more of the bait, the Ch'u swarmed into the castle and forced the Chiao to surrender.

⊛ Liu Pang's Blunder

About the time that Liu Pang, the founder of the Han dynasty, defeated his rival Hsiang Yu and established the Han Empire, an outstanding leader by the name of Mao-tun Tan-kan appeared among the Hsiung-nu,[2] a tribe of non-Chinese people in the north, and raised a powerful force of soldiers.

One year, Mao-tun led a large army and invaded Chinese territory. Liu Pang himself organized a punitive force and started off for the front. It was winter, and the battlefield was visited by a severe cold wave with unending snow. The soldiers of the Han army were stricken by the cold one after another, and two or three out of ten lost fingers.

Mao-tun was aware of this and, feigning flight, devised a strategy of luring the Han army even farther north into snow country. Liu Pang took the bait, and thinking Mao-tun had fled at to the prospect of facing a larger force, followed him north in pursuit. Mao-tun hid forty thousand elite troops to the rear, led his weaker troops on, then directed them to turn and attack the enemy. Liu Pang, who was confident of victory, had dispatched his entire mounted force in haste to the front lines to attack, leaving his foot soldiers far behind. Without a moment's delay, Mao-tun sent out the forty thousand mounted soldiers, and surrounded Liu Pang's divided force at Mount Pai Teng.

At this point, Liu Pang realized his mistake and was barely able to break through the encirclement and flee, no doubt berating himself at his carelessness in falling for a classic "Cast a Brick, Pull in Jade" strategy.

⊛ Gain and Loss Are Neighbors

We cannot simply ridicule the failures of Liu Pang. How many times have we ourselves run after some sweet bait, and then reproached ourselves for being so gullible? From the Chinese point of view, on such occasions the larger responsibility for the outcome lies with the person who took the bait rather than with he who tempted his adversary.

In a book called the *Huai Nan Tzu*,[3] it says, "Gain and loss are neighbors." And in the *Hsun Tzu*[4] we are warned, "Do not look at gain without reflecting on its concomitant loss. You should maintain a cool judgment that will be thoughtful enough to uncover a hidden loss behind the dazzle of gain."

TO CATCH A THIEF, CATCH HIS KING

擒賊擒王

摧其堅、奪其魁、以解其体。
竜戦干野、 其道窮。

Crush his armor, take his head;
thus you dismantle his body.
When a dragon fights on a plain,
he is hemmed in.[1]

If you annihilate an army's main strength and seize its leader, you can annihilate the entire army. This kind of opponent is like a dragon that has come up on land; you can defeat him in any way you like.[2]

The concept behind "To Catch a Thief, Catch His King" is that you must destroy the enemy's main strength, or his very center, to attain a lasting victory. No matter how many small, local victories you achieve, a final victory is not assured until the sustaining source of your opponent is destroyed. If you become lax before then, there is the possibility that your opponent may recover, turn on you with a ferocious counterattack, and give you a taste of defeat. To avoid this outcome, you must crush your opponent thoroughly.

What, then, is the right way to proceed? You must not be satisfied with small victories; you must pulverize the enemy's main strength and smash his will to resist. This is the strategy of "To Catch a Thief, Catch His King."

⊛ Ts'ao Ts'ao's Ready Wit

Ts'ao Ts'ao was called a crafty hero in the world of chaos chronicled in *The Romance of the Three Kingdoms*, but during his life he tasted any number of serious defeats. The following event occurred when he attacked Lu Pu, who was ensconced at Pu-yang.

From time to time, a traitor would sneak out from the castle, offering to lead in a secret attack. Ts'ao Ts'ao decided to take one man up on his offer, and, leading the army himself, approached the eastern gate under cover of night.

But just at that moment, huge flames rose up from inside the castle, illuminating the scene. Lu Pu's army rushed forth for a surprise attack. By the time Ts'ao Ts'ao realized that he had been betrayed, it was too late. His army was on its way to being completely routed.

Although Ts'ao Ts'ao had been tricked, he was a cunning leader and was able to keep his wits about him.

It wasn't long before enemy horsemen rushed in, thrust their spears in his face, and shouted, "Where is Ts'ao Ts'ao?"

"O . . . over there!" yelled Ts'ao Ts'ao, pointing at one of his generals. "The man riding that brown horse!"

As soon as they heard this, the enemy horsemen galloped after the general riding the brown horse.

With his quick thinking, Ts'ao Ts'ao himself escaped danger from his enemy, whose intent, of course, was to crush the leader and the heart of the army.

But they failed, and Lu Pu failed to follow up on his initial victory. The result of this was that four years later, when Ts'ao Ts'ao had reestablished his offensive, he destroyed Lu Pu altogether.

⊛ Strike the Weak Spot

Everything has its weak spot. There are some things so complex that you hardly know how to approach them. But if you can find the weak spot and apply pressure, your solution will be simpler than you might think. Likewise, everyone has his Achilles' heel. If you attack that, your negotiation or persuasion should go smoothly. This could also be said to be a variation of "To Catch a Thief, Catch His King."

⊛ If You Would Shoot a General, Shoot His Horse

The phrase, "To Catch a Thief, Catch His King" comes from *Before Leaving for the Front*, a poem by Tu Fu, the T'ang-dynasty poet:

> If you would shoot a man,
> > first shoot his horse.
> If you would catch a thief,
> > first catch his king.

Also most likely drawn from the same poem is the common saying "If you would shoot a general, shoot his horse," which is an interesting variation on the same theme.

The phrase is often mentioned in conjunction with a man's effort to win the heart of a young lady, suggesting that to gain the attention of your love, first make an ally of her mother. It goes without saying, however, that in our modern age, when young ladies are less attentive to their mothers' commands, this tactic loses much of its relevance.

Nevertheless, when trying to win over another person, rather than "attacking" that person directly, taking the back door and approaching someone who has influence over that person can be an efficacious strategy even today.

When planning to approach a company president, for example, there are times when approaching his wife can work wonders. This method is all the more effective in situations where the wife has her husband under her thumb.

You could say the same thing when it comes to more commercial endeavors.

When attracting customers, whom do you target? The person holding the purse strings. In Japan, this person is more often the wife than the husband. Therefore, rather than aiming for the husband (the general), most companies aim at the wife (the horse). The probability of success is higher. As a matter of fact, marketing surveys have confirmed that aiming at the purchasing desires of housewives and mobilizing these women leads to greater profits.

In broader terms, you should not be deceived by outward appearances. Yes, the general looks splendid on his steed, but if you wish to approach or attack him, seek out the true support (the horse) and aim your blows in that direction.

Part IV

STRATEGIES FOR AMBIGUOUS SITUATIONS

When offense and defense continue in a one-step-forward-one-step-back rhythm, and the tide of war becomes unpredictable, you must devise some new strategy or tactic to attain victory. In such situations, a strategy of the soft overcoming the hard may be the best way to overturn the enemy's forces.

混戰の計

PULL THE FIREWOOD FROM UNDER THE KETTLE

釜底抽薪

不敵其力、而消其勢、
兌下乾上之象。

*Do not use strength against [a stronger]
enemy, but rather wear away his vigor as in
the image of Heaven over the lake.*[1]

When the enemy's power is great, and you cannot resist with your own strength, wear away his
spirit and steal the venom from his fangs. This is
an example of forcing him to surrender by means of
"the soft overcoming the hard."

The concept of "Pull the Firewood from under the Kettle" should be applied when handling a problem by confronting the main cause does not work. But the kettle is boiling rapidly and has become unsteady, so something must be done. It is too hot to handle. If you can manage to pull the firewood out from under it, the boiling water will cool on its own, and you can easily manage the situation from then on.

In the same way, when your opponent is strong, if you face him head-on, you have no chance of winning. To destroy such an enemy, you will have to take aim at a weak point that will seal his fate. However, it is desirable that this action be relatively easy to execute and that its result be effective on a large scale.

The real problem, then, is that of finding an efficacious method. Two places of attack are as follows:

- Cutting off the enemy's supplies. No matter how great an army may be, if its supply line is severed, it will be unable to maintain its fighting strength.
- Crippling the enemy's morale. If soldiers have lost their will to act, they will not be able to function as an organization, no matter how large the force.

⊛ Attack against the Crow's Nest

The very first scene in *The Romance of the Three Kingdoms* is the Battle of Kuan Tu, in which Ts'ao Ts'ao and Yuan Shao fought for the hegemony of northern China. As Ts'ao Ts'ao gained an easy victory in this battle, he brought all of northern China under his control, and he became the main subject of the period as covered in the first half of this great epic novel.

However, the story goes that Yuan Shao's forces were far superior—twenty thousand on Ts'ao Ts'ao's side versus one hundred thousand on Yuan Shao's. With a situation like this, Ts'ao Ts'ao was at a huge disadvantage from the outset, regardless of how revered a general he was.

Ts'ao Ts'ao had repeatedly won victories in smaller skirmishes, but in the face of this large army he was now compelled to retreat little by little. His soldiers were barely able to stand their ground at Kuan Tu. It was clear that Ts'ao Ts'ao's inferior force faced an uphill struggle.

The turning point came when Ts'ao Ts'ao received a piece of information from enemy soldiers who had surrendered. According to them, Yuan Shao's military provisions were being stored in a place called Wu Ch'ao (literally, Crow's Nest), and its defenses were inadequate. As soon as he heard this, Ts'ao Ts'ao handpicked a group of highly trained troops, staged a night attack, and burned the place to the ground.

With this one blow, the tide of battle turned. Yuan Shao's army found itself without supplies. Suddenly, their resolve began to waver. Internal divisions broke out. The army fell into confusion and soon was incapable of organizing itself and preparing for battle. When Ts'ao Ts'ao's troops next attacked, Kuan Shao's army was overrun and put to flight.

◉ Breaking the Morale of the Rebels

During the Sung period, a man by the name of Hsieh Ch'ang-ju became the superintendent of Han Chou. Not long thereafter, the provincial army rebelled, took up a position in front of the official residence, and was of a mind to kill the provincial governor and the army commander. When word of this reached these two men, they began to shake with fear and would not set a foot outside.

At this point, Hsieh Ch'ang-ju volunteered to intercede. Stepping outside, he addressed the rebel soldiers thus: "I'm sure that every one of you has a father and mother, and a wife and children. Why have you done something like this? You know our leaders are like fathers to us. All of you other than the ringleaders, get out!"[2]

As a result of this harangue, all of those who had simply been following the ringleaders had second thoughts and, one by one, departed, as meek as lambs. Next, the eight ringleaders fled and hid, but each one of them was soon apprehended. Everyone in the region realized that Ch'ang-ju had averted a disaster. And how? He broke the rebel's morale by pulling the firewood from under the kettle.

⊛ The English Intelligence Corps Douses a German Fire

At the beginning of World War II, the Germans' newest weapon, the U-boat, was almost completed. Such was the reputation of the new submarine that even before construction was finished on the first group of boats, several thousand German youths had enlisted as crew members. These young men admired the submarines and volunteered in droves.

The British were alarmed, and the British naval intelligence corps, which had obtained information about this new threat, quickly commenced a counter-propaganda campaign. They printed a great number of handbills stating how dangerous it was to serve on a submarine and scattered them throughout Germany. They supported this effort by filling the German airwaves with broadcasts on how to avoid service in submarines by feigning illness.

The result was that enthusiasm for the U-boats waned, and a general aversion to the submarines became the norm. Thus, deployment was delayed for several months beyond expectations.

DISTURB THE WATER, GRAB THE FISH

混水摸魚

乘其陰乱、利其弱而無主。
随、以向晦入宴息。

Take advantage of
your enemy's internal chaos.
Benefit from their weakness and
lack of central control.
By following, you face the evening and
rest with ease. [1]

Profit from the enemy's internal confusion, a decline in his fighting strength, and any chaos in the line of command; manipulate these to your own advantage. This strategy is as natural as resting in one's home after a day's work.

"Disturb the Water, Grab the Fish" is a strategy in which you grasp victory by capitalizing on your opponent's internal disorder. If you can find no disorder, you must act to cause confusion, then take advantage of the situation.

The essence of this strategy lies in the following two points:

- You cause some disturbance to confuse the judgment of your opponent, then exploit his disorientation.
- Of the various forces and factions within your opponent's organization, you must target the section that is wavering the most.

The Strategy of Wang Yang-ming

It is well known that Wang Yang-ming, who lived during the Ming dynasty, was the progenitor of the philosophy named after him and was also one of the finest battle strategists of his time. The following occurred when he served as an army commander and suppressed the rebellion of King Ning:

Ning's forces had already opened up an assault, but Yang-ming had not yet made preparations for countering that attack, as he saw no chance of winning. Rather than fight a hopeless battle, he came up with a cunning counterstrategy. In secret he wrote the following letter to Li Shih-shih and Liu Yang-cheng, the trusted retainers of King Ning:

"You have kindly taken the trouble to inform us of your internal condition, and I am impressed with your loyalty to our court. Beyond that, I would like you to suggest to King Ning that he move to attack the enemy forces as soon as possible. If you detach yourselves from his bastion at Nan Ch'ang, everything should turn out exactly as we have planned."

This done, he dragged one of his opponent's captured spies from confinement and, choosing a spot where he could be easily seen, loudly gave an order for the man to be decapitated. Yang-ming then secretly instructed the jailor to give the spy the following message: "A fellow who admires King Ning gave me this secret letter and wants to pass it on to him." The jailor was to pass over Yang-ming's letter and set the spy free.

Once released, the loyal spy took the letter to King Ning. After reading the letter, the king was plunged into turmoil. Had two of his top men betrayed him? Was this a trick? King Ning pondered these possibilities as he considered the plan for the upcoming battle. Li Shi-shih and Liu Yang-cheng, who advocated capturing Nan Ch'ang as quickly as possible and establishing King Ning as emperor, had earlier proposed this battle. But Yang-ming's letter had sown the seeds of doubt. Was there trickery in their plan or not? Burdened with the weight of uncertainty, the king succumbed to doubt and misery.

In this way, more than ten days passed without action on King Ning's part. His advantage slipped away. Finally, King Ning discovered that his opponent's army had not yet been assembled and Yang-ming had created a clever subterfuge to play for time.

But by then it was too late.

Wang Yang-ming had confused his opponent's judgment, prepared his army, and secured a victory.

◉ Hitler's Counterattack

Toward the latter part of World War II, Hitler saw strong omens of defeat, and his decisive action for reversing this decline was the Battle of Ardennes. In December of 1944, he positioned several hundred thousand men and two thousand tanks in the hills of Ardennes, near the border of France, then set to work on a general counter-offensive.

The Germans selected two thousand officers and men who were skilled at English, dressed them in American uniforms, and gave them captured tanks and jeeps. Under this disguise, they easily infiltrated the rear lines of the American army. The disguised Germans mingled in with the American troops, then set about disrupting lines of transportation, disabling transit vehicles, cutting lines of communication, and causing general confusion. One of their units advanced as far as the banks of the Meuse River, secured the bridge, and made preparations to receive their main forces. With the stealth activity of this special corps, the line of command of the American army was temporarily thrown into great disorder.

In the end, the advance of the main German forces was kept in check, and the behind-the-lines activities these men went through such great efforts to achieve came to nothing. Hitler's move was a failure, but it nevertheless it was a classic example of "Disturb the Water, Grab the Fish."

THE GOLDEN CICADA SHEDS ITS SHELL

金蟬脫殼

存其形、完其勢、
友不疑、敵不動。
巽而止蠱。

If you preserve the form and keep the
posture, your allies will have no doubts
and your enemies will not move.
It follows that "stopping" means,
"From stagnation comes the new."[1]

Maintain the position of your camp formation, and
to the end do not ease your stance. In this way,
your allies will remain steadfast and your enemies
will not advance and attack. While sustaining your
pose, secretly move your main force.

The Golden Cicada Sheds Its Shell" is a strategy in which you make your move while giving the appearance of remaining steadfast. This strategy is highly effective if you need to retreat in the face of a great enemy force. If you are unable to continue the fight and believe that the more you hold out the more damage you will sustain, then the best plan is most likely one of temporary retreat. However, it is possible that a careless retreat will provoke your enemy to give chase and your forces could quickly be destroyed. In order to protect yourself in retreat, it is wise to give the appearance of immobility as you move. This will tie the enemy down and buy time to complete a withdrawal without incident. Prop up the shell while you empty out the center. This is the strategy of "The Golden Cicada Sheds Its Shell."

It is worth noting that this strategy is not simply one of retreat; it is also effective when you want to move without the enemy noticing.

◉ Liu Pang's Narrow Escapes

Liu Pang challenged Hsiang Yu for hegemony, but at first he found himself in a series of crises. One example is the time he was surrounded at Ying Yang. Not only was he completely surrounded by Hsiang Yu's army but he had also run through his provisions and was facing desperate circumstances. Even the resourceful Liu Pang could see no way out.

At this point, a general by the name of Chi Hsiu spoke up: "If we don't move, we'll be doing nothing more than sitting and waiting for our deaths. I'm going to distract the enemy, and while I do so, you should seize the opportunity to escape." He then presented Liu Pang with his plan.

That night Chi Hsiu dressed two thousand women in helmets and armor, and left through the eastern gate. Believing this to be a sudden counterattack, Hsiang Yu's army gathered at the eastern gate and prepared to advance.

Next, Chi Hsiu stepped into Liu Pang's chariot, pushed forward through the eastern gate, and yelled, "Our provisions are exhausted! We surrender!" The enemy generals and soldiers, fooled into thinking this was a genuine surrender, cheered and let their guard down. With that opening, Liu Pang and a number of mounted men escaped through the western gate.

When the generals captured Chi Hsiu in his master's chariot, he was brought to Hsiang Yu, who asked pointedly, "Where is Liu Pang?"

"By this time he should be gone," was the reply.

In a fit of anger, Hsiang Yu had Chi Hsiu burned alive, but Chi Hsiu's sacrifice and his artful use of "The Golden Cicada Sheds Its Shell" had allowed Liu Pang to escape unharmed.

⊚ The Sung Army's Masterly Retreat

During the Sung period, the Sung army intercepted the superior forces of the Chin but judged that if they engaged them in battle they would have no chance of victory. They thus decided to retreat, even though they were painfully aware that doing so might draw the enemy into pursuit.

The Sung found a clever solution to their predicament. They left their banners standing over the campground, suspended a number of sheep by ropes in the air, and placed large drums by their hooves. When the sheep struggled in their rope harnesses, their hooves pounded against the drums and created a great noise. Hearing the cacophony, the Chin army believed that the Sung forces were mobilizing to defend their position, and they began to ready themselves over the next several days. They marched in full force toward the Sung army, but when they finally reached the encampment they found nothing more than an empty shell. By the time the Chin had realized their blunder, the Sung army was far beyond striking distance.

⚙ The Timely Evacuation of Kiska

In the latter part of the Pacific War, Japan was beginning to sense defeat. The fierce battles with the American army on the Pacific islands were taking their toll, and their forces were being wiped out one after another. One of the most significant battles was the fight to the death on Attu Island in the Aleutian chain. The 2,576 men and officers under the command of Yamazaki Osa took a heroic stand against the landing party of 11,000 American troops, but their tragic end was inevitable. This occurred in May of 1943.

At the time of the American attack, the Japanese army also occupied Kiska, another island in the Aleutian chain. If Attu succumbed, Kiska would be next. Kiska was of meager value strategically, so the Japanese Fifth Fleet was sent to the island to assist in an immediate evacuation of Kiska's 5,639 soldiers. Unfortunately, the evacuation would have to take place right under the noses of the American air and sea forces.

The Fifth Fleet wanted to evacuate the island without alerting the Americans, but they were thwarted by a thick fog and twice failed in their rescue. The third time, however, they found a spell of clear weather and succeeded in entering the port. A further stroke of luck came when the American vessels unexpectedly departed from the area for refueling. Blessed with two strokes of good fortune, the Kiska garrison was rescued without incident to the very last man.

The Americans, however, believed the Japanese still occupied the island, and the illusion held. Two weeks later, an American force of 35,000 men invaded the small island with a decisive landing strategy. They landed in the midst of a fog, and in the absolute belief that the Japanese army was still occupying the island, the Americans engaged in a ferocious firefight with their own forces, mistaking them for the enemy. This fatal mistake was born in part from their fear of the Japanese, and in part from the general confusion caused by the extreme weather conditions. Needless to say, this tragic friendly fire incident resulted in a large number of deaths and casualties.

What the soldiers eventually discovered in the midst of the carnage were empty barracks and three lone puppies.

Bar the Door, Grab the Thief

関門捉賊

小敵困之。
剝、不利有攸往。

Intimidate a small enemy.
Splitting apart;
there is no advantage in giving chase.[1]

You can surround and annihilate a small, weak
enemy. But an enemy you have chased down may
resist and fight desperately to the end, so you
should avoid chasing him too far.

"Bar the Door, Grab the Thief" is a strategy in which you destroy an enemy you have surrounded. It can also be phrased as "catch a large haul with the single throw of a net." This strategy is the exact opposite of the one introduced earlier in Strategy 16, "If You Covet It, Leave It Alone." Where the previous strategy was indirect, this one is straightforward and confrontational.

There are two situations in which the present strategy can be put into effect:

- The enemy is either few in number or weak. This strategy should not be brought against a powerful opponent or one that is well prepared to fight. If it is used against strong opponents, it will fail.
- The enemy has the potential to cause you harm in the future if he escapes. In such a situation, you must destroy the enemy completely.

When you have surrounded a weaker enemy, you are faced with a choice: should you crush him entirely, or should you allow him to escape temporarily in the manner of "If You Covet It, Leave It Alone"? It is imperative that, in selecting a strategy, you consider the specific conditions of the case before you. Each and every case is different. However, be sure to apply the strategy of "Bar the Door, Grab the Thief" only when the rat has no fight left and will not turn and bite the cat.

The following is noted in the martial strategies of the *Wu Tzu*[2]:

Consider a single desperate thief who has fled to an open field. If even a thousand pursuers are sent out after him, it will be those pursuers who will tremble with fear. The reason for this is that the trapped thief may suddenly appear and rush in with an attack. In this way, if even a solitary thief is resolved to give up his life, he can make a thousand men tremble and shake.

In order to apply this strategy without danger, you must stifle your opponent's will to mount a desperate counterattack. You must make him think that resistance is futile, no matter what.

⊛ Pai Ch'i Destroys Evil at the Root

In the case of "If You Covet It, Leave It Alone," you judge that there is no harm in letting your opponent escape temporarily, and in fact that doing so will save further bloodshed on your side to secure a victory. On the contrary, the concept of "Bar the Door, Grab the Thief" should be applied when it is clear that letting your enemy go will only become a liability. In this case, you should not hesitate; you must strike the opponent hard and eliminate him.

The Battle of Chang P'ing—said to be the decisive battle of the Warring States period—was the first in which this strategy was applied.

In the year 260 B.C., Pai Ch'i led the 500,000-strong Ch'in army against the 400,000-strong Chao army led by Chao Kua. The two armies met at Chang P'ing. At first, Pai Ch'i feigned flight and enticed the Chao army to follow after him. He then skillfully intercepted their supply route. The result was that the Chao army was now split in two, and they soon ran out of provisions.

Chao Kua, knowing that he would have to escape, led a last, desperate charge in a pitched battle. The Ch'in army shot down his troups and Kua himself was killed. The remaining several hundred thousand Chao troops lost the will to fight and surrendered.

After the battle, Pai Ch'i deliberated on the problem of the captured Chao soldiers.

"Previously, when we captured Shang Tang," he said, "the people of Shang Tang were reluctant to become subjects of our state, and they fled to Chao. Now, although they may be Chao soldiers, we'll never know when they might betray us. We must cut this future evil at the root; we can do nothing other than to kill them all."

So saying, he had them all buried alive. Among the captured Chao, only 240 children were pardoned and allowed to return home. In a single, devastating stroke, Pai Ch'i eliminated a sizable portion of Chao's able-bodied young men and thus precipitated the rapid decline of their state's strength.

⚙ Fu Ch'a's Fatal Blunder

A decisive, unhesitating strike is the key to success in the strategy of "Bar the Door, Grab the Thief." The following is an example of how by faltering, even slightly, you invite your own downfall.

During the Spring and Autumn period, Chu Chien, the ruler of Yueh, attacked Fu Ch'a, the ruler of Wu. When the two engaged in a battle in the region of Fu Chiao, the latter won a great victory. Suffering defeat, Chu Chien organized five thousand of his remaining soldiers and made a last stand on Mount Hui Chi. However, the area was completely surrounded by Wu soldiers and there was no prospect of escape. With no other recourse, Chu Chien dispatched his chief vassal Wen Chung to sue for peace. Fu Ch'a refused, however, and Chu Chien hardened his resolve and prepared for his final battle against great odds and little hope of success.

It was at this time of desperation that Wen Chung advocated the following:

"We shouldn't be too hasty. Wu's chief vassal, Pai Pu, is an extremely greedy man, and if we bribe him, he may be able to convince his lord not to attack. Let us devise a plan in secret."

Thereupon, Chu Chien dispatched Wen Chung one more time, sending with him a beautiful woman and treasure to pass on to Pai Pu. Pai Pu was ecstatic and quickly arranged an interview with Fu Ch'a.

Through his vassal's intervention, Fu Ch'a was enticed; he changed his mind, but just as he was about to accept a peace treaty a man named Wu Tzu-hsu stepped up to object:

"If you do not deliver the final blow now, the day will surely come when you will regret it. Chu Chien is a wise ruler, and what's more, among his vassals are some remarkable men. By letting them live, you will inevitably bring trouble upon our state."

But Fu Ch'a dismissed Wu Tzu-hsu's opinion, agreed to a peace treaty, and withdrew his army. Narrowly escaping death, Chu Chien thereafter made an outward show of serving as a vassal to Fu Ch'a. In the meantime, he nursed his wounds and planned his revenge. Twenty years later, he rose up against and destroyed Fu Ch'a, finally avenging himself for the battle at Fu Chiao.

BEFRIEND THOSE
AT A DISTANCE,
ATTACK THOSE
NEARBY

遠交近攻

形禁勢格、
利從近取、害以遠隔。
上火下沢。

*When circumstances are prohibitive and
forces are at cross-purposes, profit by taking
what is nearby, and keep harm remote.
Fire over the pool.*[1]

When you have fallen into a stalemate along battle
lines, it is advantageous to attack an enemy that is
in close proximity. You should not leap over a nearby
enemy and attack a distant one. A distant enemy's
political goals may be different, but you can temporarily join hands and accomplish your task.

"Befriend Those at a Distance, Attack Those Nearby" is, as the phrase suggests, a strategy of forming alliances with distant states while attacking enemies in the nearby vicinity. If you face a number of states either resisting or confrontational toward you, the choice of whom to attack and whom to ally yourself with can make the difference between victory or defeat. At such a time, following the strategy of "Befriend Those at a Distance, Attack Those Nearby" can be highly effective. The Chinese books on military strategies—including *The Art of War*—warn against the foolishness of sending an army to a distant location. This is because such a move raises your costs, stations a portion of your forces away from your closer enemies, and has few merits. Taking the opposite approach allows one to increase his sphere of influence, expend less effort, and obtain results sooner.

◉ How the First Emperor United the Empire

The First Emperor of the Ch'in used this strategy in defeating the six states that opposed him and thereby was able to unify the empire. The story begins earlier, with the ruler Chao, three generations before the First Emperor. At that time, Chao was considering bypassing the two nearby states of Han and Wei and attacking the distant state of Ch'i. When he heard this, a man by the name of Fan Sui came forward and advocated the policy of "Befriend Those at a Distance, Attack Those Nearby," saying:

"Previously, during the time of the ruler Ming, Ch'i attacked the southern state of Ch'u, defeated the Ch'u army with a merciless attack, and extended its territory a thousand leagues in all directions. But in the end they were forced to let go of all the territory they had obtained with such pains. This was because, while attacking distant Ch'u, they allowed the nearby states of Han and Wei to build their war capabilities, thus finding themselves forced to withdraw from Ch'u and defend themselves from their neighbors.

"Surely through this example your highness can see that it would be much better to ally yourself with distant states and attack those in the vicinity. Every inch obtained is one more inch, an extension of the territory you already rule. Every foot is one more foot. To ignore this fact and attack distant Ch'i would be a grave error."

In the end, Chao adopted Fan Sui's advice as state policy and set out to rule the east. Later, the First Emperor destroyed the Han and conquered the nearby states one after another: Chao, then Wei, Ch'u, and Yen. Finally, he destroyed Ch'i and succeeded in the unification of the empire.

⊛ Diplomatic Strategy in Modern Times

"Befriend Those at a Distance, Attack Those Nearby" is also employed as a modern diplomatic strategy. Vietnam, for example, allied with the Soviet Union, both militarily and ideologically, and received aid from them. The plan behind that, needless to say, was the domination of the Indo-Chinese peninsula, while resisting heavy pressure from China. The fact that the Soviet Union gave aid to faraway Vietnam became a powerful impediment for China, which shared a border with Vietnam.

China in turn sought distant allies. In order to exert pressure on Vietnam, it began to support Cambodia and, in order to check the Soviet Union, China was even willing to approach the United States.

Castro's Cuba allied itself with the Soviet Union in order to resist America's influence; and the Soviet Union had no qualms about supporting Cuba in order to oppose the United States.

Of course, in diplomacy, the opposite approach is often employed. Allying oneself with a neighboring country in order to confront a powerful distant country has been a common tactical approach for centuries.

BORROW A ROAD, ATTACK KUO

仮道伐虢

両大之間、敵脅以従、
我仮以勢。
困、有言不信。

If a country lies between two larger ones,
and the enemy tries to subordinate it
by threats, use force provisionally
[to protect the smaller country].
If you deliver only words,
they will not be heeded.[1]

Should a small, weaker country be sandwiched between your own country and that of your enemy, and the enemy shows signs of military hostility toward that small country, then your own country must set out militarily and come to its aid, and later you can bring it under your control. If you make verbal promises but do not follow through with aid, you will be unable to gain their trust.

"Borrow a Road, Attack Kuo" is a strategy by which you take advantage of the distress of a small country and conquer it under the pretext of coming to its assistance. However, in mobilizing your army, you must justify your actions. The best opportunity for applying this strategy is when a weaker party is attacked, or there is a perceived, imminent attack by a stronger party. At such a time, you must swiftly send troops to help and thereby increase the sphere of your influence. Wait patiently for the right moment and finally conquer the weaker party. Under the guise of ostensible altruism, this strategy helps you increase your sphere of influence, while at the same time avoiding international criticism.

⊛ Breaking the Wheels of a Cart

"Borrow a Road, Attack Kuo" is taken from an event narrated in the *Han Fei Tzu*, a book by the famous Legalist philosopher of the same name. During the Spring and Autumn period, there was a large state by the name of Chin. Nearby were the two small states of Yu and Kuo.

Duke Hsien, the ruler of Chin, wanted to attack the state of Kuo.

Hearing this, one of his vassals, Hsun Hsi, suggested the following plan: "Offer the bowl of Ch'ui-chi and the horses of Ch'u as gift and request that Yu grant you passage on their road to Kuo. With the temptation of such treasures, they are sure to agree."

"Both of these are valued treasures," replied the duke. "The bowl of Ch'ui-chi is made from jade and has been handed down by former princes for generations, and the horses of Ch'u are among my most cherished possessions—swift horses for which I would gamble nothing! What will we do if Yu accepts the gifts but does not lend us the road?"

"There is no danger of that. If they do not want to grant us passage, they will not accept the gifts," Hsun Hsi replied. "If they accept the gifts and grant you passage, the gifts will be yours anyway. Think of it this way: It will be the same as transferring the jade bowl from the inner treasury to the outer treasury. As for the horses, it will be the same as tethering them in the outer stables rather than the inner ones. This is not a matter of concern."

Consenting to the plan, Duke Hsien sent Hsun Hsi as a messenger. Hsi presented the jade and horses to the duke of Yu and requested him to grant passage. The duke of Yu was exhilarated by the sight of such courtly gifts, and was set to accept the request.

Seeing this, Kung Chih-chi, a vassal to the duke of Yu, admonished him. "You must not accept this request. Our country and Kuo are two wheels on the same cart, joined by an axis. As long as the wheels are joined, the cart rolls on. The cart depends on the wheels and the wheels roll on because they are joined. In the same way, Yu and Kuo depend on each other. If you grant Chin passage, on the same day Kuo falls, Yu will fall. It would be wise to reject this request."

The duke of Yu considered the advice but chose, in the end, to disregard it.

Traveling through Yu, Hsun Hsi attacked Kuo and returned home, but three years later again raised an army, struck Yu, and destroyed it. Hsun Hsi retrieved the horses and the jade bowl and presented them to Duke Hsien.

"The gifts never truly left your possession, lord, but see how the horses have grown—they are now even stronger than when you offered them!"

Hearing this, Duke Hsien was overjoyed—the strategy of "Borrow a Road, Attack Kuo," recommended by his vassal, had been an immense success.

⊛ The Soviet Dispatch of Troops to Czechoslovakia

In 1968, the Soviet Union deployed troops to Czechoslovakia, which had been pursuing liberalization, and in a flash a requiem was said for the Prague Spring, the term for Czechoslovakia's short period of political liberation.

It all began when the Soviets staged a combined military exercise in the forested area of Bohemia inside Czech territory. Units from five countries under the Soviet Union gathered for the exercise, including those from East Germany, Poland, and Hungary.

Three months later, the Soviets, together with a vanguard consisting of the units that had participated in the exercises, invaded Czechoslovakia using a route through the Bohemia region.

Bohemia was the first "borrowed road," and the Prague International Airport was the second. A Soviet transport plane entered the airport's air space, then sent a bogus distress call, citing engine trouble, and requested permission for an emergency landing. Following international practice, the landing was permitted. As soon as the plane landed, a seventy-man armed vanguard jumped from the plane and in an instant had taken control of the airport. They then ordered the airport employees to discharge their duties and clear the way for the arrival of succeeding troops, thus securing a swift invasion.

◉ How the Underdog Can Survive

"Borrow a Road, Attack Kuo" allows the strong to conquer the weak, and—all things being equal—it should not be difficult as long as there is the will to proceed. Success relies on giving the appearance of a just cause.

Conversely, a person or country in a weak position will find it difficult to carry out this strategy. In order to avoid becoming a victim of this strategy, the following conditions must be met:

- One's interior organization must be in agreement. Internal discord and division give a strong opponent an opening he can take advantage of.

- Avoid provocative behavior. If such behavior is engaged in, it will provide the strong with the will to act.
- Be discerning about strength. Inappropriate words and actions will only buy the hatred and anger of the strong.
- Dress your intentions in diplomatic terms. In the settlement of disputes, one usually draws upon extensive diplomacy.

Part **V**

STRATEGIES FOR UNIFIED BATTLE

When allied countries unify and fight, one should not rely too heavily on one's new partners just because they are allies. You must firmly maintain leadership and manifest a strong command. You must never show an opening to either an enemy or an ally.

併戦の計

Steal the Beams, Replace the Pillars

偷梁換柱

頻更其陣、抽其勁旅、
待其自敗、而後乘之。
曳其輸也。

Force your enemy to change his formation
frequently, remove his strongest troops,
wait for him to self-destruct,
then take advantage of this.
Brake the wheels.[1]

Enervate your opponent so that he must frequently
change his battle formation and move his main
force, then take advantage of his self-destruction.
If you restrain the wheels, you are better able to
control the direction of the vehicle.

"Steal the Beams, Replace the Pillars" is a strategy in which you completely sap your opponent's strength. Beams and pillars support the structure of a house. If you take these away or alter them, the form remains in place, but the interior, or substance, will be weakened. In the same way, if you can alter the structure of your opponent's forces, his fighting ability will be lessened and he will lose the will to resist.

This strategy can be used against enemies and allies alike. It goes without saying that when this method is used against an ally, it is used in order to manipulate the other party to one's will.

⊛ The First Emperor's Strategy

The First Emperor of the Ch'in knocked down opposing states like dominoes with Strategy 23, "Befriend Those at a Distance, Attack Those Nearby," and in the year 221 B.C. he destroyed the last remaining state, Chi, finally completing the unification of the empire. During this campaign, the First Emperor used subjugation by armed strength combined with a range of strategies, which included tactics to weaken his opponents' military strength and their will to fight. He employed "Steal the Beams, Replace the Pillars" against the state of Chi.

About this time, a man by the name of Hou Sheng was appointed as the prime minister of Chi and consolidated the administrative power of the state. Determined not to allow his own hegemony to be compromised, the First Emperor set his sights on Hou Sheng. He sent him a large number of articles made of gold and succeeded finally in bribing him. Hou Sheng then complied with the First Emperor's demands to send his own subordinates and followers to Ch'in, ostensibly to learn more of the situation there. The First Emperor's people cultivated the trust of these visitors, rewarded them with many articles of gold, and sent them back to Chi as intelligence officers. In compliance with Ch'in's wishes, these men returned home, enthusiastically praised the greatness of Ch'in, and unanimously encouraged the ruler of Chi to cease his preparations for war.

Later, when the Ch'in army pressed in on the Chi capital at Lin Tzu, it is said that not one of Chi's subjects resisted. The entire state was completely subjugated without bloodshed by the activities of the intelligence agents.

⊚ The Soviet Union's Invasion of Afghanistan

For many years the Soviet foreign strategists had sought a much-desired route to the Indian Ocean, and to this end it can be argued that the Soviet Union had been preparing for the invasion of Afghanistan since the 1950s. In order to entice members from the upper echelons of Afghan society, the Soviets sent over six thousand advisors and specialists on military and governmental matters ostensibly to assist the Afghans. At the same time, they suppressed or drove out dissident factions and urged the appointment of agents friendly to the Soviet Union.

The result was that, over time, the important Afghan military and governmental agencies were almost all dominated by agents friendly to the Soviet Union. Hostile beams were replaced with friendly pillars. When the Soviets finally invaded, the initial surge was easily accomplished.

POINT TO THE MULBERRY, BERATE THE PAGODA TREE

指桑罵槐

大凌小者、警以誘之。
剛中而応、行険而順。

The great surpasses the small and
leads by means of admonishment.
To strength there will be response;
act with severity and there will be order.[1]

At times a person in a strong position must be
severe toward a weak person to bring discipline
and submission. If the stronger party confronts the
weaker one dominantly and powerfully, he will be
able to make the latter submit; approaching matters with a resolute attitude will cause your opponent to be obedient.

"Point to the Mulberry, Berate the Pagoda Tree" is fundamentally a method whereby you want to criticize A (the Pagoda Tree), but you hesitate to face him directly and so rebuke B (the Mulberry Tree). In this way, you criticize A indirectly. This strategy has been frequently used since ancient times. Some years ago, for example, there was a movement known as "Strike Lin Piao, Strike Confucius." While this movement outwardly criticized Lin Piao and Confucius, it was really aimed at criticizing the politician Chou En-lai.

This strategy can also be used to bring around a friendly state or subordinate. That is to say, at times when it would not be efficacious to criticize a friendly state directly, or a subordinate unsparingly, "Point to the Mulberry, Berate the Pagoda Tree" could be a useful alternative.

⊛ Sze Ma Jang-chu's Impeccable Organization

During the Spring and Autumn period, there was a general in the state of Chi by the name of Sze Ma Jang-chu, who left for posterity the famous book *The Art of Sze Ma*, one of the *Seven Books on Martial Strategies*.[2] When Chi was attacked by the state of Yen, Jang-chu was appointed general, and his troops prepared to depart for the front. During this time, a court favorite by the name of Chuang Ku was appointed as an army inspector, and he periodically accompanied the troops. However, on the day the troops were due to leave for the front, Chuang Ku showed up extremely late.

"What kind of excuse do you have for being so late?" Jang-chu demanded furiously.

"I'm so sorry!" was the answer. "The major vassals and my relatives came to bid me farewell, and so I was late."

Hearing this, Jang-chu sent for the authority on martial law in his army and asked him, "According to martial law, what kind of sentence is given to a person who is late for an appointment of such importance?"

"Beheading is appropriate," the man replied.

Chuang Ku was struck with fear. After sending a runner to inform the ruler of his plight and request support, he begged for mercy. But before his messenger could return, Jang-chu executed Chuang Ku and announced the punishment to the entire army.

It is said that, in the shadow of this incident, army discipline improved in an instant.

While it is uncertain exactly why Jang-chu made such an example of Chuang Ku, in terms of efficacy he certainly achieved strict military discipline by "Pointing to the Mulberry, Berating the Pagoda Tree."

However, one cannot win the minds of subordinates with discipline alone, and during the campaign, Jang-chu was an exemplary leader. He assisted in many chores most commanders would leave to underlings, helping with everything from tidying the soldiers' quarters to drawing well water and stacking cooking pots and provisions. He ate the same rations as the lowliest soldier and in the same amounts. He even attended to ill soldiers. In this way he proved he could show a kinder, more sympathetic side to his men.

By being both strict and humble, Jang-chu made a reputation for himself. After only three days, when it came time for roll call, even the sick soldiers asked to go to the front and faced battle in high spirits.

◎ Striking a Balance between Severity and Sympathy

While the Japanese possess a strong loyalty to the group ethic, the Chinese focus more on the individual. A Chinese manager attaches importance to discipline—that is, showing their subordinates a severe demeanor. But you cannot win your subordinates' hearts with severity alone. What is also necessary is *jin*, or "human-heartedness"—that is, sympathy and understanding. Without exception, people who are called wise generals are those who strike a balance between severity and human-heartedness.

While the group ethic plays an important role in Japanese society, the Japanese have an intense dislike of confrontation, and if this dislike manifests itself as avoidance of responsibility within an organization, management will find it necessary to introduce a corrective dose of strictness into the proceedings.

Creative solutions have been found to overcome this aversion to confrontation. When energizing a professional baseball team, for example, a Japanese manager might first obtain consent from one player in private and then deliberately make an example out of him by singling him out for a scolding, even if the blame lies more with other members of the team. The manager will single out a designated scapegoat to indirectly criticize the entire team. If that player is the captain of the team or a veteran, this plan works all the better, and it becomes a creative version of "Point to the Mulberry, Berate the Pagoda Tree."

FEIGN STUPIDITY, DO NOT BE INJUDICIOUS

仮痴不癲

寧偽作不知不為、
不為作假知妄為。
靜不露機。雲雷屯也。

Feign a lack of knowledge and do not act,
rather than dissembling with borrowed
knowledge and acting indiscriminately.
Be at peace, and do not manifest your
intention. Clouds and thunder indicate
Birth [or difficulty at the beginning].[1]

Rather than trying to be clever and acting carelessly
and indiscriminately, it is better to deliberately look
foolish and refrain from action. While you hide
cunning plans in your breast, do not manifest them
on the exterior. This is exactly like clouds and thunder accumulating their strength and waiting for the
right moment to unleash the storm.

"Feign Stupidity, Do Not Be Injudicious" is a strategy in which you give the appearance of being quite foolish, which disarms your opponent's vigilance. "Stupidity" means "foolishness," while "injudicious" means "to be mad." Therefore, "not injudicious" means "having normal judgment." Based on these nuances, "Feign Stupidity, Do Not Be Injudicious" is nothing less than a stratagem in which you cloak yourself in foolishness, a tactic often used by those in a weak or desperate position. If it is executed well and successfully, it can be a highly beneficial strategy, but the key to making it a success hangs on the quality of a person's performance when feigning stupidity.

⊛ Sze Ma Chung-ta's Masterly Performance

In *The Romance of the Three Kingdoms*, Sze Ma Chung-ta, who was Chu Ko K'ung-ming's worthy opponent, later became a meritorious retainer and elder statesman to the ruler of Wei, for whom he played a leading role.

During that time, the influence of Ts'ao Shuang, the scion of an illustrious family in the court, came to the fore; and Chung-ta, who had been pushed aside and held no real power, temporarily pleaded illness and shut himself up in his mansion. Nevertheless, Chung-ta remained an elder statesman of the ruler of Wei.

Ts'ao Shuang and his coterie were making their influence felt, and to them Chung-ta's existence was threatening and thus intolerable. Ts'ao Shuang therefore sent an underling as a messenger to Chung-ta, instructing him to spy on Chung-ta under the guise of asking after Chung-ta's health.

When the messenger was brought before Chung-ta, what he saw astonished him. Two young ladies stood at either side of Chung-ta, assisting him in the simple act of dressing. When his clothing seemed about to fall from his shoulders, they would quickly adjust his robes. Chung-ta pointed his finger at his mouth and mumbled incoherently "Ah . . . oo . . ." to the young ladies, apparently asking for a drink.

When the young ladies offered a tea bowl filled with gruel, he tried to take a sip but spilled it all over his chest. He was unable to answer any questions at all.

The messenger returned and reported to Ts'ao Shuang: "Lord Chung-ta was totally incoherent, and he was unable even to sip gruel. I think that it will soon be the end for him. You have nothing to worry about."

Ts'ao Shuang was put completely at ease and thought no more about Chung-ta.

One month later, Chung-ta exacted his revenge, capitalizing on Ts'ao Shuang's negligence, to execute a coup d'état, destroying them and all other opposition, and making a comeback to his seat of power. His strategy of "Feign Stupidity, Do Not Be Injudicious" was a resounding success.

◉ When the Charade Fails

The third-generation Ming-dynasty ruler was Emperor Yung Luan. He was the fourth son of the dynasty's founder, Chu Yuan-chang, and was called "the epitome of wisdom and courage" from the time he was young. Among his brothers, he enjoyed a reputation as the most remarkable.

Recognized for his abilities at an early age, Yung Luan was quickly given the position of the ruler of Yen, stationed in Beijing, and ordered to keep an eye on the movements of the Mongols. Soon afterward, Chu Yuan-chang died in the capital of Nanjing, and Emperor Chien Wen was enthroned as the second-generation ruler. The new emperor was nephew to Yung Luan of Yen.

From the start, however, the relationship between the court of Nanjing and the ruler of Yen in Beijing lacked harmony, and it soon became one of opposition. Yung Luan was the emperor's uncle, and this created tensions in their relationship. Furthermore, he commanded a major military force, was stationed in Beijing, and was hugely popular. If the emperor let matters stand, he knew Luan would one day become a threat to the court in Nanjing. Thus, it was desirable to eliminate his uncle and contain this potential disaster before it grew worse. As a countermeasure, the emperor sent a trusted retainer and high official to consolidate his surveillance in Beijing.

For the ruler of Yen, such a move by his opponent could not be ignored. The strategy that he chose to combat the emperor's move is echoed in a passage in the *History of the Ming*: "The ruler, himself aware of the internal danger, feigned madness and pretended to be ill." In other words, "Feign Stupidity, Do Not Be Injudicious."

He soon put the strategy to work. Sometimes he would go into the streets of Beijing, take food and drink away from people, shout absurdities along the way, and act like a lunatic. At other times he would start up a fire on a hot midsummer day and begin to shiver, mumbling, "Oh, it's cold, it's cold."

All will be fine if your opponent is fooled by your performance, but if your charade is uncovered, the consequences could be disastrous. In Luan's case, his pretense was less than convincing, and the emperor's vigilance increased. The result was that the internal feud between nephew and uncle proliferated into a battle of relatives in which blood was washed with blood.

As wise as the man who later became Emperor Yung Luan was, he was not cunning enough to make this strategy a success.

◉ The Copper Coins

Playing the fool requires a detailed plan. This is at the heart of this tactic, and the following story illustrates a clever variation.

This event occurred when Ti Ch'ing had embarked on a campaign to defeat a non-Chinese tribe in the south. At that time in that region, the practice of divination was popular among the Chinese and carried great sway.

Recognizing the power of divination, Ti Ch'ing decided to exploit it. He took out one hundred copper coins and in front of his soldiers said, "In the coming battle, victory or defeat is completely unpredictable. So I will throw these coins in the air, and if they *all* come up heads, that will mean the gods are behind us and we are sure to win."

Everyone knew the odds of such a feat occurring naturally were so low that only divine intervention could make this happen.

A staff officer at his side whispered, "If they don't come up heads, it will have a devastating effect on the morale of the troops," and tried to dissuade him, reasoning that this was a hugely foolish act.

Ti Ch'ing, however, could not be swayed. As a large crowd of soldiers looked on apprehensively, he threw all of the copper coins in the air. As they fell to the ground, every last one of them turned up heads. Seeing this, the entire army, generals included, burst out in hearty cheers of joy.

Ti Ch'ing nailed the copper coins down just as they were and, after covering them with a cloth, said in a commanding voice, "If we make a triumphant return, we'll give thanks to the gods." His troops immediately turned to the battle lines and annihilated the rebels.

After their triumphant return, the staff officers inspected the collected coins, only to find that each coin had heads on both sides. Behind their leader's seemingly rash pronouncement had been a cleverly devised strategy.

SEND THEM TO THE ROOF, REMOVE THE LADDER

上屋抽梯

仮之以便、唆之使前、
断其援応、陥之死地。
遇毒、位不当也。

If you fool your enemy with deceptions,
entice him to advance, and cut off his access
to help, you will put him in a fatal situation.
He encounters poison, his position crumbles.[1]

Draw an opponent in, deliberately enticing him
with an opening and cutting off the troops that
follow. Then surround and annihilate him. The
enemy brings about his own downfall by lunging at
the bait you left.

"Send Them to the Roof, Remove the Ladder" is the strategy of sending an opponent to a position you can control and then isolating him. It can also be used to motivate your own troops. As a military strategy, it could follow one of two patterns:

- You throw out bait that the enemy is likely to take, let him rush in recklessly, and cut him off from any further troops or collaborators.
- Make your troops stand with their backs to a body of water so there is no possibility of retreat, strengthen their resolve by showing them victory is the only way out, and send them to battle in high spirits.

In both cases, this is a strategy that requires considerable resolve to succeed. It is essential to have deep insight and make meticulous preparations.

One other concern with this strategy is the plan that you use to entrap your rival. Make sure it is foolproof. Even today, this is a valid strategy.

◉ Li Lin-fu Eliminates a Political Threat

During the T'ang period, there was a prime minister by the name of Li Lin-fu who served the emperor Hsuan Tsung. He was said to have "a mouth of honey, but a sword in his stomach." In other words, Lin-fu excelled at intrigue. Among his political enemies was a man by the name of Yen T'ing-tze, who had been demoted to serving in the provinces.

Once, during a conversation with Lin-fu, the emperor suddenly recalled the talented Yen T'ing-tze and inquired after him. "Ah, yes. There was a man by the name of Yen T'ing-tze, wasn't there? He was an able fellow, but where is he now?"

After promising to make inquiries, Li Lin-fu withdrew and summoned T'ing-tze's younger brother, hatching a plan that would eradicate any further threat from his rival.

"The emperor is keen to meet your brother again. I think that perhaps we should bring him back from the provinces. What do you think? How about making a request, saying that he would like to return to the capital to recuperate on the grounds of having developed palsy? I think you should recommend this to your brother."

Yen T'ing-tze was contacted by his brother and happily drew up a letter to the throne as suggested by Lin-fu, requesting his return to the capital.

The emperor consulted Lin-fu as to what this was all about.

Lin-fu replied, "T'ing-tze is not getting any younger and has developed palsy. I think it would be best if you order him into retirement and have him concentrate on taking care of himself."

In this way, Li Lin-fu successfully eliminated any political threat from his rival, demonstrating an artful political use of the strategy "Send Them to the Roof, Remove the Ladder."

◉ "Break the Ovens, Sink the Boats"

In the military laws of *The Art of War*, the following tactic is mentioned as a means for motivating your soldiers to fight:

> Once you have given soldiers a mission, cut off any road of retreat as if you had sent them up to the second floor of a building and then removed the ladder. If you have penetrated enemy territory deeply, you must advance like an arrow released from a bow. To urge your soldiers onward, burn the boats, break the cooking pots, and make the soldiers abandon any hope of returning home alive.

Hsiang Yu was among those generals who made a specialty of this way of fighting. He followed this approach when he came to the aid of his allies, the Chu Lu, who were surrounded by the armies of the Ch'in. He led his entire army to the front, then as soon as they had crossed the Yellow River, he sank their boats, destroyed their cooking ovens, burned their tents for bivouacking, and brought along only three days' worth of provisions. Taking such extreme measures, he sought to give the generals and soldiers alike no hope of returning home alive. Facing such nihilistic consequences, the soldiers would have no choice but to fight with desperate resolve.

In the end, Hsiang Yu's soldiers hurried to the side of their ally, and each man fought as though he would subdue ten of the enemy. They fought with such fierceness that enemy and ally alike could barely catch their breath.

This is called Hsiang Yu's strategy of "Break the Ovens, Sink the Boats," and it is, of course, a practical application of "Send Them to the Roof, Remove the Ladder."

◉ K'ung-ming's Severed Supply Lines

Hsiang Yu's strategy, developed by Hsiang Yu himself, realizes great power when a decisive, short-term battle looms, but it is less effective in long-term, ongoing fights.

The former Japanese Imperial army often employed the same tactic. It can be said that from the outset, however, the Japanese army had a tendency to underestimate the importance of supply communications. Furthermore, they did not make a distinction between a short-term and a long-term campaign in many of their battle strategies. Employing strategies that often ignored supply lines during the Pacific War led to tragedies like the one at Imphal.[2]

The crucial tactical distinction between short- and long-term campaigns, as well as the vital role of supply lines, was not lost on Chu Ko K'ung-ming, as told in *The Romance of the Three Kingdoms*.

When Liu Pei died, K'ung-ming received his last blessing, executed a series of far-reaching campaigns of grand design, and challenged his rival, the state of Wei, to battle. This battle, he realized, would be a hard, long-term struggle. The reasons for this were twofold. First, Wei was a large state with many times the resources of K'ung-ming's state of Shu. Second, to strike at Wei territory, it was necessary to traverse high mountains called the Ch'in Ling Range. Naturally, securing supplies would be extraordinarily difficult.

K'ung-ming had the resources for an army and strategic leadership, but the difficulties of building sustainable supply lines over a forbidding mountain range in those days—even for a resourceful man like K'ung-ming—were hard to surmount. This obstacle would prove too great for even such an intelligent leader as K'ung-ming to overcome.

Knowing he was at a disadvantage, K'ung-ming proceeded cautiously. He did not attempt the impossible. Whenever his supply lines were disrupted, he called for a temporary retreat, recuperated his troops' strength, and prepared for the next battle. He would forget about implementing his strategy of "Send Them to the Roof, Remove the Ladder," and replace it with a tactic known as "Tap a Stone Bridge, Then Cross."[3]

K'ung-ming was ultimately unable to reach his goal. However, neither was he defeated. For a fundamentally inferior force such as K'ung-ming's, it is possible to say that the very fact they survived and put up such a spirited fight is in itself a small victory. This is more than can be said for the Imperial Japanese army in the wake of the Pacific War.

⊛ Remove the Ladder, Light a Fire

Honda Performance and Research, an arm of the Honda Motor group, is well known as a company that challenges itself to come up with new products that appeal to the younger generation. Furthermore, it is known for encouraging its employees to be creative. Some years ago, it developed the "City," a "tall but short car" that broke with the conventional wisdom about car design that had prevailed up to that time. The man who developed this concept was one of the youngest men on the team, whose average age was twenty-seven.

Management had promised not to interfere with this young project team. Nevertheless, as well as having a free hand to create, the designers had to assume various responsibilities for the project.

When asked about their approach, management replied as follows: "When you give work to researchers, you are generally severe, but sometimes you slacken the rope. When you do this, there will be a considerable spike in the number of ideas that come forth. It is good to watch these things carefully and to let them accumulate. This should be done haphazardly, however, and in certain situations you must be resigned: assign standards and responsibilities, and then say nothing after that. Take them to the second floor, and then remove the ladder; after that, they cannot jump down, even if you tell them to. Is it not true that our creative ideas flourish when forced into extreme circumstances?"

If you follow the same line of thought, so the theory goes, you will surely be able to draw out one hundred percent of the potential possessed by the young generation. There are those, however, who criticize Honda Performance and Research's way of doing things as "taking them to the second floor, removing the ladder, and starting a fire beneath them."

MAKE THE FLOWERS BLOOM ON THE TREE

樹上開花

借局布勢、力小勢大。
鴻漸于逵、
其羽可用為儀也。

Take what you can from the situation,
and pave the way for your influence;
though you have but little strength,
your influence will be great.
The wild goose gradually progresses
over the broad highway;
its feathers can be used for ceremonies.[1]

If you feign superiority, you can demonstrate great power, even if you are equipped with but a small and weak military force. Look at the wild goose that flies through the sky. Does it not spread its wings wide and manifest magnificent spirit?

"Make the Flowers Bloom on the Tree" is a strategy in which you feign great military strength. *The Art of War* advocates withdrawing if your force is weak. "Make the Flowers Bloom on the Tree" affirms that confrontation should be avoided but also suggests that, in some cases, you could strike a pose of military superiority and trick your enemy into submission. But whether you retreat or feign strength, the underlying point remains the same: avoid fighting for a while and play for time.

⊛ The Cooking-Oven Strategy of the Eighth Route Army

In Strategy 15, "Pacify the Tiger, Then Lead It from the Mountain," we introduced an example in which a weaker army nightly increased the number of cooking ovens to make it appear as though reinforcements were arriving in preparation for battle. In its war of liberation, the Eighth Route Army tried a similar strategy against the army of the Kuomintang, the Chinese Nationalist Party.

In the winter of 1947, the Ch'en Keng regiment of the Eighth Route Army, which was active in guerrilla warfare in the Fushan area of western Henan Province, found themselves facing the superior force of the Kuomintang, and for a short time needed to avoid them. Rather than retreat, they formed a plan to distract the enemy. They created a decoy unit whose sole purpose was to drag the Kuomintang on a wild goose chase.

This unit was under instructions to give the impression that they were the Eighth Army's main force. The decoy unit feigned a sortie and then commenced a cat-and-mouse strategy of dragging their opponents around. The decoy unit started south in full view of the enemy, and as soon as they were convinced the enemy could no longer see them, they doubled back and marched south on the same road, creating the impression of a larger force. When camped, they made a great number of campfires to give the appearance of a large regiment

The enemy was not so easily drawn in. The decoy unit thus changed tactics and attacked the prefectural garrison at Chen Pei, deliberately creating the impression that this was a sortie of the main force. When reports of the scale of the attack reached the enemy forces, they sent out their main force and moved aggressively toward a decisive battle.

The decoy unit withdrew, dragging the enemy farther and farther away from the main force of the Eighth Army, and then pulled away from them. Even then they did not let up. They marched along, creating billowing clouds of dust suggestive of a much larger force; they left behind a disproportionately large number of rucksacks; and they carried out other actions that gave the impression of a large army on the move. Though initially skeptical, in the end the Kuomintang were taken in by the deceptions and believed the decoy unit to be their opponent's main force. They thus chased them for a number of months. During that time, the main force of the Eighth Army was able to enjoy a long rest and prepare for the decisive battle that was soon to come.

⊛ The Soviet Union's Strategy of Deception

In his *Battle Strategies of Modern Times*, Nagai Yonosuke introduces the following episode:

In the beginning of the 1970s, reconnaissance satellite cameras over Soviet airspace discovered an increase in submarines carrying intercontinental missiles. These submarines were part of the Soviet northern fleet stationed in the port of Polyarny in the vicinity of Murmansk. For a number of days, however, violent winds had been blowing in the Barents Sea, and the surveillance cameras had not been functioning well. Once the winds had passed and the cameras were working again, Western operators were surprised to observe that half of the new submarines had been damaged in the winds, their hulls twisted or capsized. The operators then deduced that the submarines could not be made of steel. The storm had exposed the submarines as dummies—the Soviets had been employing the strategy of "Make the Flowers Bloom on the Tree" to magnify the strength of their fleet.

This was indeed the case. Years later, a former high-ranking engineer in the Soviet war plant explained that it was his responsibility to make fake weapons out of wood. "They looked just like the real thing from a distance," he related. "A special building was constructed for their manufacture, and the surroundings of the plant installations were completely camouflaged." On the island base of Saaremaa opposite the port of Riga, there was a great number of real missiles, but thanks to this engineer's efforts, the number of imitation missiles exceeded the number of real ones. The tactic's two-pronged approach created false impressions of the size of the fleet and of the location of its major force.

After relating this episode, Mr. Nagai commented, "Of course, this sort of deception had only the tactical intention of deceiving and confusing the West. However, even on a strategic level, this point can be considered: The Soviet Union had hidden its real strength for the past thirty years, and in order to inflate their real strength they took extreme measures."

QUIT AS GUEST, TAKE OVER AS HOST

反客為主

乘隙插足、扼其主機。
漸之進也。

Take advantage of an opening,
insert your foot, and grasp the main chance.
Advance is in gradual progress.[1]

If your opponent gives you an opening, capitalize on it immediately and grasp power. This must not be carried out in an arbitrary fashion, however. The correct procedure must be followed, and your goal must be accomplished step by step.

"Quit as Guest, Take Over as Host" is a strategy in which a person in the position of follower (guest) takes over the seat of leader (host). That is to say, the party that was initially in a passive role seizes control. In terms of battle, *The Art of War* states that it is essential to secure leadership and to impose one's own pace on the enemy. If one remains in the "guest's" position, he will never hold a position of leadership. This is the meaning of "Quit as Guest, Take Over as Host."

In order to realize this strategy, the following procedure should be followed:

1. Secure the guest's seat.
2. Search for the host's weak points.
3. Initiate action.
4. Seize power.
5. Change positions with the host.
6. Solidify power.

While one remains passively in the guest's seat he must not behave rashly but rather must be patient and circumspect and wait for the right time to strike.

⊛ Liu Pang's Patience

Hsiang Yu and Liu Pang each led their own army corps as generals affiliated in the anti-Ch'in alliance, and each took his own route to the Ch'in capital at Hsien-yang. Among the armies of the alliance, Hsiang Yu's corps was the main force, and Liu's Pang's was a detached force. Ironically, however, despite being the weaker force, Liu Pang's corps was the first to attack Hsien-yang. General Hsiang Yu was furious at Liu Pang's audacity. Venting his anger, he decided to attack Liu Pang.

At this time, Liu Pang's troops numbered one hundred thousand men while Hsiang Yu's forces stood at four times that number. Clearly, Liu Pang had no chance of victory.

Seeing no alternative, Liu Pang set off for Hsiang Yu's camp, accompanied only by an attendant, to apologize. This famous event in Chinese history is known as "The Meeting at Wild Goose Gate." Liu Pang's servile act was certainly a wise move. He would not have been able to overcome Hsiang Yu by force, so he opted for humility and loss of face.

Not long thereafter, Hsiang Yu became the de facto leader. As the postwar map was being drawn and the land being divided, the inner circle of the military alliance had decided that the general who first attacked Hsien-yang would be awarded the Land within the Passes (Shensi). This, of course, was Liu Pang. But the alliance withheld this desirable region from Liu Pang, instead awarding him a remote scrap of land called Han Chung. With this brazen insult, Liu Pang's patience broke. Enraged at the blatant unfairness, he made ready to go into battle. But his advisers were adamant—now was the time for patience, as his army was in no position to secure a victory. Liu Pang was ultimately swayed by their compelling argument, relinquished his plan, and headed grudgingly toward Han Chung.

Liu Pang secluded himself in remote Han Chung and waited. Eventually his patience paid off, and an opening presented itself. He swiftly exploited Hsiang Yu's shortcomings, raised an army, removed him from power, and claimed the empire for his own.

While in isolation, Liu Pang demonstrated a meticulous patience and circumspection, qualities that are essential to success with "Quit as Guest, Take Over as Host."

◉ Circumspection and Tenacity over Three Generations

When Sze Ma Chung-ta was young, he was highly regarded as an able and intelligent man. One man he clearly made an impression on was Ts'ao Ts'ao of Wei, who was rapidly rising through the ranks of power at that time. Indeed, after Chung-ta was discovered by Ts'ao Ts'ao, it was decided that he would serve in Wei. Even from the outset, however, it seems that the relationship between the two did not go well.

When Chung-ta was still attached to Prince Ts'ao P'i, Ts'ao Ts'ao had a dream that he became convinced was some sort of premonition. In it, three horses had their heads thrust into the same manger. Shortly after having this dream, Ts'ao Ts'ao said to Ts'ao P'i, "There is the possibility that our clan will be usurped by Chung-ta, so be very careful of that man."

Because this came from Ts'ao Ts'ao, his discomfort could have been interpreted as "make sure this man dies soon," indicating Ts'ao Ts'ao's trust in Chung-ta had begun to wane.

Chung-ta, however, while under the watchful eye of Ts'ao Ts'ao, waited on Ts'ao P'i hand and foot and performed his duties diligently. Gradually, Ts'ao Ts'ao's vigilance began to fade, and over time Chung-ta's stature rose. Eventually, with Ts'ao Ts'ao's death, Ts'ao P'i took the throne, and Chung-ta was satisfied to be his trusted retainer. After Ts'ao P'i's death, he became a highly regarded, senior vassal to the Wei kingdom's court.

Chung-ta, however, began and ended his career as a vassal. The next generation benefited from Chung-ta's exalted position. But it was with his grandson, Sze Ma Yen, that the Sze Ma clan usurped the Wei court and established the Chin court.

In the end, the Sze Ma family realized the strategy of "Quit as Guest, Take Over as Host" over three generations.

Part VI

STRATEGIES FOR A LOST BATTLE

Even when you find yourself in a desperate situation, it is ill-advised to resign yourself to fighting to the bitter end. Wherever there is a will, there is a way. There are any number of secret strategies for retaliatory victories. When the situation turns dire and defeat looks more and more likely, it is best to flee. Today's judicious retreat can lead to tomorrow's victory.

敗戦の計

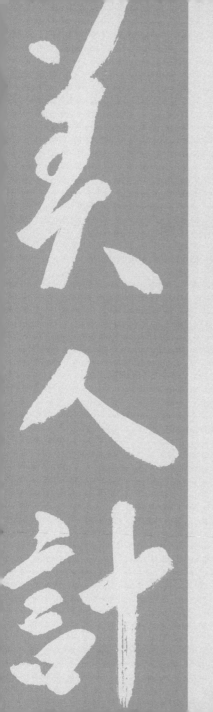

THE STRATEGY OF THE BEAUTIFUL WOMAN

美人計

兵強者、攻其將。
將智者、伐其情。
將弱兵頹、其勢自萎。
利用御寇、順相保也。

When an army is strong, strike at its general.
If the general is wise, attack his spirit.
If the general is weak and the army is
coming apart, its power will wither of itself.
It is beneficial to suppress the enemy;
this is pliability and concomitant protection.[1]

Facing an enemy of great military strength, it is best to cajole its commander. If the opposing commander is wise, devise a strategy that will weaken his will. If you deprive both the commander and the soldiers of their will to act, your opponent will collapse internally. If you can take advantage of your opponent's weaknesses and manipulate him freely, you will be able to turn the tables to your favor and exploit him to your will.

The "Strategy of the Beautiful Woman," as the title suggests, originally involved the use of a beautiful woman to lure the opponent's thoughts away from political or military battles. In the *Lu T'ao*, a book on the martial arts, it states, "Bribe him with an abundance of jewels; amuse him with beautiful women." And: "By inserting the lascivious voice of a beautiful woman, you can lead him astray." Essentially, the point of this strategy is to beguile your opponent and to weaken his drive, thereby depriving him of his will to act. Although this strategy is largely employed by a weak person against a stronger foe, it can, of course, be used in the opposite situation as well.

⊛ Chu Chien Entices His Opponent

Toward the end of the Spring and Autumn period, Chu Chien, the ruler of Yueh, was forced to sign a humiliating peace accord at Mount Hui Chi after being defeated by Fu Ch'a, the ruler of Wu. He was pardoned and allowed to return home, but his pride had suffered a demoralizing blow, and he vowed never to allow himself to forget the taste of defeat at Mount Hui Chi.

Determined to redeem his honor, Chu Chien began a twofold plan in preparation for revenge.

First, he revolutionized the government of his own state. Learning from his former inexperience, he reconstructed the state administration and strengthened the armed forces. He reorganized agricultural labor and invited men of talent from far and wide to come to Yueh.

Second, while strengthening his own state's power, he sought means to undermine Fu Ch'a's. He devised a plan to use a beautiful woman to seduce and entrap his rival.

In order to successfully lure Fu Ch'a, the woman would need to be blessed with a singular charm and exceptional beauty. Quickly issuing a notice throughout Yueh, he was able to find a beautiful young woman by the name of Hsi Shih, the daughter of a wood seller who lived at the foot of Mount Chu Lo. Despite her remarkable beauty, however, Hsi Shih was a country girl and lacked all the manners required of a lady of the court. Chu Chien brought her to the capital and had her trained in all the arts of a modern lady, from conduct and manners to makeup and style of walking. This rigorous curriculum lasted for three years, such was Chu Chien's insidious, synchronizing need for revenge.

When she had mastered all the decorum and attained the polished grace of a lady, Hsi Shih was sent to Wu and given an audience with Fu Ch'a. No sooner had Fu Ch'a set eyes on her than he became hopelessly infatuated, and he immediately took her as a concubine. His infatuation was to cost him greatly. Blinded by this feminine treasure, Fu Ch'a began to lose his sense of vigilance and neglected the affairs of Chu Chien. Fu Ch'a had become ensnared by the "Strategy of the Beautiful Woman," and all the while Chu Chien had been waiting for his moment. When it arrived, Chu Chien exacted his revenge mercilessly and destroyed him.

◉ Freed by a Beautiful Woman

During the reign of Chou of the Yin, there was among the various minor nobility a character by the name of Hsi Pai. While Chou was considered a tyrant, Hsi Pai ruled his state admirably and was popular among his peers. Aware that Hsi Pai's popularity might pose a threat, one of Chou's advisers confided, "Hsi Pai practices good government and has won the hearts of his peers. If you don't dispose of him soon, it could spell bad tidings for the future."

Chou thereupon seized Hsi Pai and placed him under house arrest. Hsi Pai's subordinates, seeing their master's life was in danger, quickly took action. They scoured the land for beautiful women, exceptional horses, and various precious articles and goods, which they presented to the ruler through one of Hsi Pai's vassals.

Upon receiving such kingly gifts, Chou was delighted and said, "With such gifts as these, there is no reason not to pardon Hsi Pai."

He thereupon released Hsi Pai and allowed him to return to his former land.

Though not an overt political or military victory, Hsi Pai's freedom had nonetheless been restored by his subordinates' use of the "Strategy of the Beautiful Woman."

Interestingly, much later, Hsi Pai's son, the ruler Wu, destroyed Chou and established the Chou court.[2]

⚙ The Power of a Beautiful Woman

The "Strategy of the Beautiful Woman" had more uses than simply seducing an enemy into carelessness. It could also be a useful tool for espionage and assassination. While such clandestine activities are not well recorded in Chinese history books, beautiful women were often sent as spies or assassins masquerading as concubines to the opponents.

The story of the Fragrant Queen helps illustrate the effectiveness of this strategy. At the time of the Ch'ing emperor Kan Lu, there was a queen by the name of Hsiang Fei. She lived in a tribe of Mongols in the regions bordering western China. Her name meant "Fragrant Queen," and as her title implied, she was a beauty who always exuded a wonderful fragrance. When the emperor Kan Lu heard of her legendary beauty, he decided that he had to have her. He thereupon sent a punitive force to the western regions, killed the entire tribe, and took Hsiang Fei captive.

Winning her favor, however, proved a harder feat, and she would listen to nothing he said. At length she pulled a naked blade from her sleeve and pointed it at the emperor. Unwilling to be seen fighting a woman, Kan Lu backed down and ordered the older courtesans to disarm her.

Hsiang Fei laughed and remained defiant. "You're wasting your time," she said. "I have ten more inside my robes."

Her resolute will only fed the emperor's lust, and he grew even more infatuated by Hsiang Fei. Her defiant nature had won the emperor's love, but it was to prove a double-edged sword. As time passed, the emperor's mother grew ever more concerned that she could become a threat, until finally, without her son's knowledge, she had her assassinated.

The story of the Fragrant Queen demonstrates how a woman's beauty can be more powerful than the mightiest army and can gain access to quarters even the most cunning of foes cannot enter. Perhaps Hsiang Fei did not desire to kill the emperor, but she would likely have had any number of chance had she wanted to. Her story is a fine reminder of how potent and lethal the "Strategy of the Beautiful Woman" can be.

THE STRATEGY OF THE EMPTY FORTRESS

空城計

虛者虛之、疑中生疑。
剛柔之際、奇而復奇。

*The weak show weakness and
create yet more doubt in an already
doubting opponent.
When this is a matter of the weak against
the strong, this yields wonderful results.*

When your own defense is inadequate, if you give
the appearance of being completely defenseless,
you will be able to muddle the enemy's judgment.
This strategy should be used when you are militarily inferior, and it can have unexpected results.

When your forces are inferior and you have no chance of victory, the "Strategy of the Empty Fortress" is a psychological tactic in which you brazenly display your defenselessness to such an extent as to confuse the enemy's judgment. The aim of this strategy is not to gain a victory over the enemy but to buy time and forestall the enemy's attack. This is often used when you are facing a last-stand situation. That is, you are looking for a life-saving strategy in the midst of a crisis that will only lead to death if drastic measures are not taken.

The "Strategy of the Empty Fortress" comes from a famous episode concerning the commander Chu Ko K'ung-ming in *The Romance of the Three Kingdoms*. Though this episode is fictitious, the strategy itself was sometimes used in real battle with success.

⊛ K'ung-ming's "Strategy of the Empty Fortress"

When he heard that his advance guard led by Ma Shu had been utterly defeated by Chung-ta, K'ung-ming immediately commanded his entire army to retreat. At the same time, he himself retreated to Hsi Ch'eng and brought along provisions. During that time, an uninterrupted flow of messengers on fast-moving horses traveled between encampments as K'ung-ming nursed his army's wounds and tried to plan his next move.

K'ung-ming presently received information that the enemy commander, Chung-ta, was leading an army of 150,000 men and advancing on the garrison at Hsi Ch'eng.

Unfortunately, any attempt to fight would mean an unmitigated rout for K'ung-ming—he had only a meager 2,500 soldiers inside the garrison. The staff officers all turned pale on hearing the news, but K'ung-ming immediately ordered, "Lower the banners! Everyone go up into the watchtowers and man your posts, but do not show yourself. I will cut down any man who draws attention to himself!"

With this command, he opened up the fortress gates on all four sides and ordered twenty soldiers to dress as civilians and sweep the road around each gate.

He then gave his next instructions with great care: "Listen closely! Even if the Wei soldiers approach, do not raise an alarm. No matter what."

K'ung-ming himself discarded his armor and disguised himself as a Taoist. He took a five-string lute under his arm and, accompanied by two youngsters, ascended the fortress tower. He then lit incense and began to play the lute.

When Chung-ta reached the fortress walls, the eerie silence that greeted him threw him into confusion.

Presently, he shouted, "Withdraw! Withdraw!" and ordered the entire army to retreat.

His son, Sze Ma Chao, who waited at his side, said, "Father, the forces inside the castle are clearly inadequate, so isn't K'ung-ming doing this intentionally? What are you thinking of, by withdrawing the army without going on the offensive?"

Chung-ta replied, "No, no. I know K'ung-ming, and he is a deeply cautious character. He would not risk danger to this extent even once. His throwing open the fortress gates like this is a thinly veiled trap, and I am convinced that there are soldiers inside lying in ambush. If we attack now, it could be our undoing. We must leave as fast as we can."

Chung-ta's army withdrew like a receding tide. When K'ung-ming's astonished generals and soldiers inside the castle asked how he had thought of this strategy, K'ung-ming replied, "Chung-ta knows me well, and believes me to be a man who does not take risks. So when he saw the unguarded fortress, it wouldn't have entered his wildest thoughts that I would have gone into hiding and left our garrison vulnerable. No, he had doubts and feared an ambush, and so he withdrew his soldiers. As for me, I was not happy to put us at risk, but I did so because it could not be avoided."

This story is the prototype of the "Strategy of the Empty Fortress." We must treat the strategy with some healthy caution, however, as this episode is, after all, fictitious.

⊛ Chang Shou-kuei's Bluff

There are very few instances of a successful application of this strategy. One example is the case of Chang Shou-kuei, whose story bears a striking resemblance to the tale of his fictional counterpart.

During the rule of the T'ang-period emperor Hsuan Tsung, a non-Chinese tribe called the T'u-fan (Tibetans) invaded the province of Kua and killed the commanding officer of the garrison there. The T'ang court thereupon appointed a man called Chang Shou-kuei as the new commander.

After taking up his new appointment, the first thing Shou-kuei did was to take charge of the locals and commence with the repair of the fortress walls. Before he was able to complete this task, however, the T'u-fan returned in force. With repairs and preparations incomplete, a successful defense was impossible. Knowing this, the locals were thrown into a panic.

Chang Shou-kuei stepped forward and said, "Not only are we vastly outnumbered but we are also unprepared militarily. This is a grave situation—we desperately need a strategy to make the enemy retreat."

So saying, he ordered a drinking party on the fortress walls, accompanied by a musical troupe, and had everyone join in riotous merrymaking.

The T'u-fan army encircled the fort, but when they saw the festivities they grew suspicious. They became convinced their attack had been anticipated and believed soldiers were waiting in ambush inside the fortress. The bluff worked: the T'un-fan army soon withdrew, and Shou-Kuei's people were spared a massacre.

CREATE A RIFT

反間計

疑中之疑。

比之自内、不自失也。

Bring doubt upon doubt.
Know your own people well so you will not
lose to this ploy.[1]

Create the dark demon of doubt within the enemy
and muddle his judgment to the very end. Effectively use your opponent's spies and you will obtain
victory without effort.

"Create a Rift" is a tactic in which you circulate false information and disrupt the enemy's judgment. Using the enemy's spies against him is considered one of the most effective means of circulating misinformation.

According to *The Art of War*, there are two basic methods for using the enemy's spies: either buy them off so that they will disseminate your own propaganda, or set out false information for them to "discover." Both of these are classic methods for this strategy.

◉ Sowing the Seeds of Doubt in the Enemy's Top Ranks

Liu Pang's troops were surrounded by Hsiang Yu's superior army and thrown into some bitter fighting. Faced with mounting odds, his staff officer, Chen Pei, came forward with this advice:

"The incorruptible knights who follow Hsiang Yu really number no more than several commanders under his strategist Fan Tseng. We should prepare gifts of ten thousand pieces of gold, send out some spies, break up the relationships between our opponent's princes and vassals, and plant in them the seeds of mutual doubt. Hsiang Yu is emotional and easily deceived, so this will surely cause some internal discord. If you then take advantage of this rift and attack, you will surely be able to destroy him."

Liu Pang agreed to Chen Pei's plan, immediately prepared the gifts of gold, and handed them over to his officer. "Use these," he said. "You have been a loyal adviser, and so I entrust this task entirely to you."

Chen Pei sent the money out, then dispatched his spies to spread various rumors among the upper ranks of Hsiang Yu's military. A common deception he instructed his spies to spread was the following: "Hsiang Yu's commanders have performed great and meritorious deeds. However, because he cannot award them fiefs to compensate for these deeds, they are ready to abandon him for Liu Pang."

Hsiang Yu heard these rumors and began to harbor grave doubts about his commanders. He sent a messenger to Liu Pang in the hope of uncovering more. Chen Pei prepared an elaborate banquet for the messenger, had princely men serve him, and even prepared a ceremonial tripod kettle, normally reserved for only the most distinguished of guests. Just as they were about to eat and the messenger had formally introduced himself, Chen Pei glanced up at the messenger's face with what appeared to be surprise.

"What? You've been sent by Hsiang Yu? I thought you were Lord Fan Tseng's messenger."

This said, he quickly took away the elaborate meal, dismissed the servants, and instead offered him some rather meager food.

As soon as Hsiang Yu's messenger returned to camp, he reported the details of his reception. This affront to his messenger was enough to provoke Hsiang Yu to entertain doubts about Fan Tseng. These demons would not leave Hsiang Yu, and his doubts became so unrelenting that his trust in his chief strategist rapidly eroded, to the point where he would no longer take any advice Fan Tseng gave at all. Angered and insulted, Fan Tseng abandoned Hsiang Yu and withdrew to his hometown.

In this way, Chen Pei used the strategy of "Create a Rift" to undermine his opponent's upper echelon, and Hsiang Yu's army was gradually driven out by an inferior force.

⊛ What the Spies Overheard

During the Sung period, the general Yo Fei was ordered by the court to pacify the Ling Piao rebels. The rebel chief, Ts'ao Ch'eng, however, would not easily submit, so Yo Fei ordered a military offensive.

When Yo Fei's army had advanced as far as the province of Ho, they captured some rebel spies. Yo Fei had these men bound and then thrown to the ground near his tent. He then emerged from his tent and, apparently unaware of the nearby prisoners, asked his subordinates for a report on his army's remaining provisions.

The official in charge responded, "We are almost out of provisions, sir. What shall we do?"

Yo Fei's face was resigned. "There's nothing we can do," he said. "We'll have to withdraw as far as Ch'a Ling."

As Yo Fei spoke these words, he suddenly glanced at the spies. Feigning surprise and unease that his situation may have been compromised, he quickly retreated to his tent. He then gave secret instructions to allow the men to escape. When the spies returned, they reported the conversation to Ts'ao Ch'eng. Undoubtedly relieved to hear this news, Ts'ao Ch'eng relaxed and dropped his guard.

Meanwhile, after allowing enough time for this false news to penetrate the enemy camp, Yo Fei quickly had provisions prepared, secretly ordered the mobilization of his troops, and advanced along the valleys. Just before dawn he launched a sudden attack on Ts'ao Ch'eng's unsuspecting troops and annihilated them without mercy.

⊛ A Portrait Condemns Its Subject

This event occurred when the founder of the Sung dynasty, Chao K'uang-yin, attacked the Southern T'ang. On the side of the Southern T'ang there was a formidable general by the name of Lin Jen-chao. He was a strong and resourceful leader, and the opponents of the Southern T'ang were unable to defeat his troops.

Finally, Chao K'uang-yin thought up a strategy. He first bribed one of Lin Jen-chao's attendants and had him secretly procure Lin's portrait. He then seated the attendant in a special room and conducted an audience with a messenger from the Southern T'ang.

Showing the messenger the portrait, he asked, "I suppose you know who this is?"

The messenger replied, "Is it not a portrait of our state's general, Lin Jen-chao?"

Chao K'uang-yin nodded solemnly then said, "Jen-chao has petitioned for surrender. As a token of his intentions, he has sent this portrait." As he spoke, he pointed to a detached mansion on the grounds. "We have come to an agreement on his terms of surrender. That is the place where Jen-chao will live."

The messenger quickly reported this incident to the ruler. Completely taken in by the ploy, the ruler became enraged and ordered Lin Jen-chao assassinated by poison. K'uang-yin's strategy of "Create a Rift" had successfully duped his enemy and afforded him the satisfaction of seeing one of his deadliest military adversaries destroyed from within.

The Strategy of Self-Injury

苦肉計

人不自害、受害必真。
仮真真仮、間以得行。
童蒙之吉、順以巽也。

Ordinarily, you do not inflict injury on
yourself, but if you plan to do so for
strategic purposes, the injury must be real.
If you can dissemble and make that
dissemblance believable,
you'll be able to carry off your plan.
The good fortune of the foolish youth:
he follows orders, and thus is docile. [1]

People do not normally invite harm on themselves
or their allies. If harm is inflicted, it usually occurs
due to the actions of a second party or due to circumstances beyond their control. But if inflicting
an injury on yourself or one in your party carries
strategic benefits, it must be done in a convincing
manner in order to succeed. To make a believer
out of your opponent, you must deliver a true
performance.

The "Strategy of Self-Injury" is one in which you inflict pain upon yourself in a manner that thoroughly convinces your enemy. It is essential that you are ruthless enough to deceive even your own allies. The story below is taken from *The Romance of the Three Kingdoms,* and in it the Wu commander Huang Kai supposedly used this strategy at the Battle of the Red Cliffs. Today this story is thought to be more invention than fact, but the strategy itself has been used in real battles since ancient times, often with great success.

⊚ Huang Kai's False Surrender

This event is alleged to have occurred during the period of the Three Kingdoms, when the navy led by General Chou Yu attacked Ts'ao Ts'ao's large army in the area of the Red Cliffs.

Seeing Ts'ao Ts'ao's large warships moored on the opposite shore, the commander Huang Kai approached Chou Yu and said, "The enemy has a large army which our forces cannot repel. As things stand, we cannot hold out for long. The enemy warships anchored on the opposite bank, however, are attached to one another bow to stern. This makes them vulnerable, so if we launched a fire attack at those ships, we could cripple them."

Chou Yu agreed enthusiastically, so Huang Kai immediately procured a number of ships and made preparations for a fire attack. At the same time, they secretly devised two further strategies to guarantee the success of the attack.

First, they would send a messenger to Ts'ao Ts'ao suing for surrender. They knew, however, their opponent would not be fully convinced by this gesture, so they devised a second tactic. In this one, they would use the "Strategy of Self-Injury."

Taking his seat at the strategy conference, Huang Kai passionately advocated surrender. Chou Yu vehemently protested, incurring the wrath of Huang Kai, who sentenced his subordinate to be whipped one hundred times. When Chou Yu was dragged back to the encampment, the flesh on his back was ripped and he was covered in blood. His injuries were so severe that it was said he lost consciousness. This news inevitably found its way to Ts'ao Ts'ao, through his spies. The ruse had worked—initially, Ts'ao Ts'ao had been suspicious of Huang Kai's offer of surrender, but now he was convinced.

When Huang Kai's flotilla finally drew near Ts'ao Ts'ao's fleet, his guard was down, believing they had come to surrender. The flotilla moved within easy striking range, then unleashed a deadly attack, utterly decimating Ts'ao Ts'a's warships. Chuo Yu had paid for this victory with his own blood, but it was a masterful use of the "Strategy of Self-Injury."[2]

⊕ Li Hsiung's Willing Victim

The following event transpired during the period of the Northern and Southern Courts. When Li Hsiung of the Later Shu was attacked by the Chin army led by Lo Shang, Li's vassal P'o T'ai expressed a different opinion and was whipped terribly. P'o T'ai then rushed to Lo Shang and, after showing him his terrible wounds, made this proposal:

"Now I bear a grudge against Li Hsiung and would like to secretly defect and join hands with you. When I return to the fort, I will send you a signal. When you see a burst of flames from inside the fort, it will be time to attack."

P'o T'ai's wounds were grievous indeed, so Lo Shang had no reason to doubt P'o T'ai's falling out with Li Hsiung. Believing he had found a secret ally, he instructed his officers to ready the entire army for a general attack, then had them follow after P'o T'ai.

Meanwhile, however, anticipating that Lo Shang would fall for the trap, Li Hsiung had placed an ambush by the side of the road that led up to his fortress. Li Hsiung's soldiers hid and waited for Lo Shang's attack. When P'o T'ai arrived back at the fort with Lo Shang's troops not far behind, he climbed the fort walls on a rope ladder and lit a blazing fire. Lo Shang's troops promptly began to ascend the fortress wall in the same manner, but P'o T'ai suddenly drew up the rope ladders and cut down more than a hundred men. Lo Shang barely had time to realize he had been duped before Li Hsiung ordered his entire army to break the ambush and attack. They caught Lo Shang's army from the front and rear and utterly annihilated them.

⊕ Duke Wu's Ill-Fated Vassal

"The Strategy of Self-Injury" involves sacrificing or injuring something that is important to you in order to gain victory or strategic advantage. It is a ruthless strategy, but precisely because of its cruel nature, it is highly effective, as the following story illustrates:

This occurred when Duke Wu of Cheng was seeking to conquer the Tartars. He first sent his own daughter to the king of the Tartars, offering her hand in marriage. The king accepted, and an ostensible alliance was formed.

Later, during a meeting with his vassals, he declared his intention to expand his influence and asked them their opinions on which nation would be most expedient to attack first. His major vassal, Kuan Ch'i-ssu replied, "I think the Tartars would be a good target."

Duke Wu was incensed. "My own daughter is married to their king! We are allies!" he yelled. In a stark example of the duke's unswerving ruthlessness, he promptly had Kuan Ch'i-ssu executed.

When this incident was reported to the king of the Tartars, he was put completely off guard, and, convinced he would not be attacked, abandoned all of his preparedness against Cheng. Duke Wu's coldblooded sacrifice had achieved its purpose, and in that unguarded moment, he mobilized an army and took the Tartars by storm.

THE STRATEGY OF LINKS

連環計

将多兵衆、不可以敵。
使其自累、以殺其勢。
在師中吉、承天寵也。

It is foolhardy to attack an enemy who has
many generals and a great number of troops.
Get them tied up amongst themselves,
and you will weaken their strength.
The commander is there,
and in the center; good fortune.
He receives Heaven's favor. [1]

When the enemy has great military power, it is
unwise to challenge him in a frontal attack. In
order to secure victory, first it is essential to devise
a strategy that will cause the enemy soldiers to
hinder one another and thus weaken themselves. If
your own commanders use such a strategy, you can
take the victory.

"The Strategy of Links" is a tactic in which you cause the enemy to trip over his own feet and thus weaken him. It is an early strategy designed to irritate the enemy psychologically, thus paving the way for a following strategy of attack. In this way, this strategy combines several tactics in sequence, first causing internal disruption, which sets the conditions for external annihilation. It is not a strategy that aims at a single, clear victory; its distinctive features are that it first confines the opponent's movements and then moves in for the kill.

◉ P'ang T'ung's "Strategy of Links"

According to The *Romance of the Three Kingdoms*, during the Battle of the Red Cliffs, a military strategist named P'ang T'ung, who was fighting for Liu Pei, approached the enemy, Ts'ao Ts'ao, under false pretenses to offer advice. A sizable part of Ts'ao Ts'ao's navy was inexperienced and unaccustomed to life at sea. Many of his men were suffering seasickness, and even Ts'ao Ts'ao himself was experiencing headaches. P'ang T'ung sought to exploit this to Liu Pei's gain. Acting as an impartial adviser, he suggested to Ts'ao Ts'ao that his flotilla of warships be chained together, and that planks be fixed above the chains to allow easy access from ship to ship. This, he argued, might give at least some semblance of life on land, and thus alleviate the crew's sickness somewhat.

Ts'ao Ts'ao was so frustrated with the situation that he immediately embraced the idea and had his men work on attaching the ships from bow to stern. This would prove to be fatal, however, as the ships became sitting ducks for Huang Kai's deadly fire attack, as recounted in Strategy 34. While binding the warships together may have provided temporary relief for the crew, the move had effectively shackled the fleet, practically offering victory on a plate for Huang Kai's subsequent surprise attack.

Thus P'ang T'ung's true intention was revealed: he had employed "The Strategy of Links" to bind the enemy's movement, create confusion, and help secure an easy victory for Huang Kai's fleet.

⊛ Destroying a Superior Enemy

The Sung court fell victim to numerous invasions by the powerful Golden Hordes,[2] and in the various battles and skirmishes that ensued, the court was often exposed as the inferior force. Nevertheless, a number of notable generals within the court employed some masterful strategies and eventually broke through the superior might of their enemy. One such general was Pi Tsai-yu.

Tsai-yu's basic battle strategy was simple in conception. If his opponent advanced first, he would retreat; if he observed them retreating, he would advance. Avoiding direct battle, he would gradually wear his opponent down, then employ guerrilla warfare tactics to strike at them. One such battle occurred when fighting the Golden Horde. After a period of characteristic taunting, the enemy forces were losing patience. Aware that cracks were beginning to show, Tsai-yu devised a plan to immobilize his enemy's forces, thus affording him a relatively easy counterattack.

Under cover of night he took a large quantity of beans that had been boiled with aromatic ingredients and scattered them on the ground some distance from his forces. With that, he embarked on his trademark carrot-and-stick tactics to entice the enemy to attack, luring them toward the area where he had scattered the beans. The Golden Horde promptly chased after him. By the time the battle commenced at dawn, their horses were famished. When they smelled the aroma of the beans, they proceeded to devour them and would not budge even when whipped. With the enemy forces effectively paralyzed, Tsai-yu executed a violent offensive and obliterated the Golden Horde's forces without mercy.

His "Strategy of Links" had created internal turmoil, incapacitating the enemy troops and thus paving the way for a lethal counterattack.

⚙ The Three Arrows

It is said that "To take initiative is to control others," and this adage was common at the time when Hsiang Liang and Hsiang Yu raised armies against the Ch'in. Indeed, the benefits of taking the lead and establishing one's dominance cannot be underestimated. Taking an early initiative puts one in the best possible position to achieve one's goals.

Getting a head start is not enough in itself, however. What follows is just as important. Consider when one fires an arrow at an enemy. While the first can deal an initially devastating blow, if it is not followed up swiftly by the second and third arrows, the enemy may only stagger, and the final, lethal blow may not be delivered. This is also true in boxing. The "one-two punch" maneuver requires follow-up punches after the initial blows. Stopping with the initial combination is insufficient; it is in the subsequent follow-up blows that the real damage is inflicted.

When you take the initiative in battle and attack first, it is desirable to be prepared with a second and third strategy up your sleeve. Furthermore, in order for your strategies to be successful, it is essential that you remain adaptable. Flexibility and adaptability are the cornerstones of effective battle strategy; without these, it is impossible to react to unforeseen changes and you will be unable to unleash your second and third arrows.

Retreat Is Considered the Best

走為上

全師避敵。

左次無咎、未失常也。

The entire army avoids the enemy.
There is no blame in retreating
and taking shelter.
Doing so, one will not yet have lost
his ordinary condition. [1]

This strategy is about withdrawing the entire army and avoiding the enemy's attack. In desperate circumstances, one must always be ready to retreat—this is an incontrovertible law of battle.

This tactic advocates the idea that the very best strategy is to avoid a fight. In the Chinese books on the martial arts, there was from the beginning no such military concept of an "honorable death" as in the image of a shattered jewel.[2] Rather, as in "Retreat Is Considered the Best," there was a fundamental recognition that you must not fight if you have no chance of winning.

For example, in the *Sun Tzu* it says, "If you have an inferior military power, retreat; if you have no chance of winning, do not fight."

And in the *Wu Tzu* it says, "If you see the benefit, attack; if you see no benefit, it is essential to retreat."

This may come across as common sense, but there are innumerable historical examples in both ancient and modern times of defeats following absurd battles.

History is replete with unremarkable commanders who knew how to advance but consistently failed to retreat even against immeasurable odds. The Chinese call such people "rank and file men" and have no respect for them. What is desired of commanders and men responsible for organizations is not simply the courage to advance, but the courage to recognize when the task is overwhelming and to retreat graciously.

What merit, then, is there in retreating? First, though you may not win, you certainly do not lose. Put another way, you, avoid unnecessary damage. Second, you can preserve your troops' strength and prepare for the next battle.

◉ Liu Pang's Flight

It is said that any man who has accomplished great things does not hesitate to take flight if the situation demands it, and that his flight is achieved gracefully and with finesse. Liu Pang of the Han, who destroyed Hsiang Yu and took control of the empire, was one of those men. In the early years when Liu Pang challenged Hsiang Yu for hegemony, his forces were constantly pummeled by Hsiang Yu's superior army, and he suffered many humiliating defeats. But Liu Pang was a shrewd commander, and he never once committed rash acts or forced his army into untenable situations. When he saw he had no chance, he would retreat and avoid the brunt of Hsiang Yu's onslaughts. For this reason, his army was always able to return to the battle line.

Liu Pang's strategy was far from one of cowardice. Despite military defeats and constant retreats, his counterstrategy was twofold: in retreat he was able to concentrate on maintaining his supplies and create a net of encirclement around Hsiang Yu's troops. Despite Liu Pang's withdrawals, his army was never truly demoralized, nor was it ever ruined beyond repair. By keeping his army afloat, when the tides of battle eventually turned to his favor, he was able to capitalize on this and grasp an unexpected victory over Hsiang Yu. This would never have been possible had he not masterfully executed his many timely retreats.

⊕ Ts'ao Ts'ao's Chicken's Rib

In The *Romance of the Three Kingdoms* Ts'ao Ts'ao is often depicted as a merciless, malevolent ruler, but in reality he was one of the most remarkable men of his age. He was an extremely effective operator on the battlefield, securing the vast majority of victories in the many battles with his rival Liu Pei. His martial planning had a number of distinctive features. First, he intensely studied such books on the martial arts as *The Art of War*, and mastered the fundamental strategies and tactics taught there. Moreover, even if faced with an unforeseen loss, he was skilled at adapting quickly to the circumstances. Next, if he suffered a temporary defeat, he would learn from his lesson and avoid making the same mistake twice. Furthermore, when he judged he could not secure victory if he attacked, he would retreat quickly and without hesitation.

An example of one of Ts'ao Ts'ao's timely retreats occurred when he was engaged in fierce fighting with his nemesis, Liu Pei, at Han Chung. Liu Pei was encamped in a stronghold there and had mounted a formidable defense. Ts'ao Ts'ao's forces were having a desperate time trying to breach their foe's lines, but they wouldn't break. Ts'ao Ts'ao presently judged the situation to be hopeless. Realizing further fighting would only debilitate his army's strength, he gathered his staff one evening and yelled at them "This is a chicken's rib! You understand? A chicken's rib!"[3]

His staff at first had no idea what he meant, and they thought he might be losing his mind. However, one of them, by the name of Yang Hsiu, promptly began preparations for a withdrawal. When the others asked why he was doing this, he replied, "Chicken's ribs are things you hesitate to throw away, even though there's barely any meat on them to eat. This battle at Han Chung is exactly that, a chicken's rib. It is of little gain to us, yet we cannot seem to end this folly. It occurred to me that Ts'ao Ts'ao wants us to retreat."

Soon after, Ts'ao Ts'ao abandoned Han Chung and returned to his capital. Far from regretting this defeat, he was relieved he could return with his army intact. Weighing up the value of the territory of Han Chung and the loss he would incur in trying to gain it, he chose withdrawal, an affirmation of the strategy "Retreat Is Considered the Best."

⊚ Know When Retreat Is the Better Option

Formerly we Japanese were bombarded with the notion that to show your back to the enemy is cowardice, or to retreat is to lack self-respect. Nowadays such views are not so prevalent, but nevertheless they still seem to be deeply rooted in the Japanese psyche and are hard for us to ignore. In fact, the Japanese have never been much good at running away at all.

On this point, conversely, the Chinese are experts. When they see that conditions are unfavorable, the first thing they do is consider flight. Their philosophy is that if one escapes temporarily, he can preserve his fighting strength and return when conditions are more propitious. It is possible to see this as a quintessentially Chinese concept.

Where did this difference arise? One could do worse than consider that the answer lies in the concept of space. China is a vast nation. So vast, it is relatively easy for tens of thousands—even hundreds of thousands—of soldiers to hide themselves in, making the prospect of a safe escape all the more likely. From this point of view, running away is a perfect strategy; in fact, it would be foolish not to do so if faced with overwhelming odds.

A small, narrow country like Japan, on the other hand, is not conducive to effective military retreats, as there is limited space in which to run. Even a single criminal on the run, like Kunisada Chuji,[4] is unable to evade the police for long. With the prospects for escape severely limited, a military philosophy that advocates fight over flight is almost inevitable, hence the high esteem in which concepts like "Be hit and shattered like a jewel" are held.

This is not to say that such concepts are without merit. Standing your ground can lead to heroic and unexpected victories. But there are times, of course, when it can lead to a crushing defeat and the entire army shatters like a jewel. And when the jewel is shattered, it cannot be mended.

To remain alive in this chaotic world, one must attack when it is best to attack and make a total withdrawal when it is best to retreat. The wisdom to know which is best to apply is the key to a successful, intelligent life.

NOTES

TRANSLATOR'S PREFACE

1. Yamamoto Kansuke (?–1561) was the legendary strategist and castle architect for the warlord Takeda Shingen. The historical record of Kansuke is almost exclusively limited to Obata Kagenori's *Koyogunkan*, and he is thought by some historians to be a fictional character. He is said to have died at one of the battles at Kawanakajima. Kansuke later became a favorite subject of professional storytellers and popular art and literature.

2. Takeda Shingen (1521–73) was the great warlord of Kai province (now Yamanashi Prefecture) who, through strategic prowess and a disciplined army, expanded his holdings and began a campaign to control the capital at Kyoto. He was considered by many the most likely warlord to unify the country and establish a new shogunate, but he died, either due to a disease or by an assassin's bullet fired during the siege of a castle held by Tokugawa Ieyasu. It is said that on hearing of his death, Uesugi Kenshin, Shingen's perennial opponent on the battlefield, lamented that he had lost the very best of his enemies.

3. The *I Ching* is considered to be the world's oldest book, having been compiled some three thousand years ago. It has been used variously as an oracle and as a practical guide for living in the world, studied intently by Taoists and Confucians alike. Each chapter of the *I Ching* is based on one of sixty-four hexagrams and contains a Judgment, an Image, and comments on each of the six lines of the chapter's hexagram. Confucius and his disciples appended additional commentaries around the fifth or sixth centuries B.C.

Strategy 1: Obscure Heaven, Cross the Sea

1. "The *San kuo chih yen i* [*Romance of the Three Kingdoms*], attributed to one Lo Kuan-chung, is an historical novel based upon the wars of the Three Kingdoms [220–265], which fought for supremacy at the beginning of the third century A.D. It consists mainly of stirring deeds of warfare, of cunning plans by skillful generals, and of doughty deeds by bloodstained warriors. Armies and fleets are

from time to time annihilated by one side or another—all this in an easy and fascinating style, which makes the book a joy to old and young alike. If a vote were taken among the people of China as to the greatest among their countless novels, the *Romance of the Three Kingdoms* would indubitably come out first." From Herbert A. Giles, *History of Chinese Literature*

2. The Yellow Cap Rebels, or the Yellow Turbans, were so called because of the yellow head cloths worn by their members. Their rebellion broke out in the province of Shantung in eastern China in 184 A.D. and spread as far as Honan. Known as the "Way of Great Peace" (T'ai P'ing Tao), it was led by faith-healing Taoist priests and continued to cause great devastation for three decades.

3. The Chinese character 城 (*ch'eng*) is variously translated as fortress, city, or castle. During the periods covered by this book, it could have meant either a walled city or a fortress; it would not likely have been a castle as we envision them in Europe or Japan. For consistency's sake, I have translated the word as "fortress" throughout.

4. The Chinese character 王 (*wang*) is generally translated as "king," but this may be misleading to Western readers. During its early history, China was broken up into a number of independent states, the rulers of which were titled *wang*. But if China is considered as a whole, like France or England, the term "king" may be confusing as there was no king of China; unified China was ruled by an emperor. For this reason, I have translated *wang* as "ruler," except in the case of titles, such as "King Chuang" or "King Ning."

Strategy 3: Borrow a Sword to Make Your Kill

1. Ts'ao Ts'ao of Wei, Liu Pei of Shu, and Sun Ch'uan of Wu—these were the three main rivals for hegemony during the Three Kingdoms. After years of hardships, Liu Pei prevailed and became the founder of the Shu Han dynasty.

2. One of Liu Pei's "Three Paladins" (the others being Chang Fei and Chu Ko-liang). Kuan Yu was later apotheosized as the god of war, and his image is commonly used for statues, *netsuke*, etc., to this day.

3. *Han Fei Tzu* is a book by an author (d. 233 B.C.) of the same name, possibly the prince of a royal family. His writings are described as "Legalist" or "Realist," but he seems to have been somewhat influenced by Taoism. The book has been compared to Machiavelli's *The Prince*.

Strategy 4: Await His Tired Steps at Your Leisure

1. From the 41st hexagram, *Sun*, of the *I Ching*, or *Book of Changes*. In the Commentary, it states:

   Decrease. Decrease that which is below, increase that which is above; this is the way upward. Decrease with sincerity leads to fundamental good fortune without blame, but one should be sincere. There is benefit in having some place to go. How can this be put into use? Two small bamboo bowls may be used for consecration, which means they may be used appropriate to the moment. There is a time to *decrease the hard and increase the soft*. Increase and decrease, fullness and emptiness—all of these go along with the moment.

Strategy 5: Take Advantage of the Fire to Plunder the Goods

1. From the 43rd hexagram, *Kuai*, from the *I Ching*. In the Commentary, it states:

   Resolution is to have made your decision. *The hard [yang] will scatter the soft [yin]*. Be vigorous and joyful, decisive and undisturbed. To proclaim this publicly is the soft [yin line] riding on the five hard [yang lines]. There is misfortune in shouting out your sincerity because when danger comes, it will be clear and bright. Reveal this from your own territory. There is no benefit in engaging in battle; too much respect for arms will bring you to a standstill. There is benefit in having some place to go; if the hard continues long enough, the matter will come to an end.

2. Ch'in Shih Huang Ti, referred to hereafter as the First Emperor, was the man who unified China by conquering the states of Han, Chao, Wei, Ch'u, and Ch'i. He became emperor in 221 B.C., and applied the laws and domestic systems of his state of Ch'in throughout China. Considering the writings of the philosophers, including Confucius and Lao Tzu, to be subversive, he or one of his ministers enacted a great "Book Burning" in 213; he banished or executed philosophers who would not recant. The First Emperor was an extremely severe ruler, and although he thought his empire would last ten thousand generations, the Ch'in dynasty survived only until 206 B.C., just four years after his death in 210.

3. After the fall of the Ch'in dynasty, Liu Pang was one of the contenders for the imperial throne, despite his less-than-aristocratic origins. Although not a strong force at first, he was patient and circumspect, and eventually became emperor, founding the Han dynasty. He is generally known as Kao Tsu (High Progenitor); the Chinese refer to themselves as the "people of Han" to this day.

4. Hsiang Yu was the main contender for the imperial throne after the death of the First Emperor. He was said to be over six feet tall, charismatic, and quick to eliminate his allies if he deemed it expedient. After a long series of battles, his once-superior forces spent, he was defeated and killed by the armies of Liu Pang, and he famously cried out in death that it was Heaven that had defeated him.

5. *The Book of Poetry* (*Shih-ching*) is one of the Confucian "Five Classics." *The Book of Poetry* contains 305 poems of varying themes, collected from the tenth to the seventh centuries B.C. Confucius considered this book to contain the best of human emotions and their expressions, and he stated that it could be summed up with the phrase, "No twisted thoughts."

Strategy 6: Be Heard in the East, Strike from the West

1. Indicates the forty-fifth hexagram, *Ts'ui*, of the *I Ching*. In the Image, it states, "Earth below, the Lake above. The Gentleman will polish his weapons, and take care not to be confused."

Strategy 8: Cross over to Ch'en Ts'ang in the Dark

1. From the forty-second hexagram, *Yi*, of the *I Ching*. The Commentary states:

> *Increase* lessens what is above and increases what is below. The people rejoice without limit. From above, it goes down below; its way becomes tremendously bright. It is beneficial to have some place to go. Hitting the target and correct, it is joyous. "There is benefit in crossing a great river" means that the boat will move along its course. *Increase moves and then follows through*; it proceeds forward day-by-day without limit. Heaven administers and Earth gives birth; thus the method of increase [of the Ten Thousand Things]. Generally, the Way of Increase proceeds in accordance with the moment.

Strategy 9: On the Distant Shore, Watch for Fire

1. From the sixteenth hexagram, *Yu*, of the *I Ching*. The Commentary states:

> As for *Enthusiasm*, the hard [yang] responds [to the numerous yin], and carries out its will. *With order, motion is enthusiastic. Enthusiasm with order moves*, and thus Heaven and Earth are like this. All the more, then, will subordinates be established and armies moved. With order, Heaven and Earth move; thus the moon and the stars make no mistakes, nor do the four seasons go off course. With order, the holy man moves; therefore crimes and

punishments are clear, and the people submit to this. The moment and significance of Enthusiasm are great indeed.

2. A fisherman's benefit. The full phrase is, "Bird and shellfish locked in a fight is to the benefit of a fisherman."

3. *Nurete de awa* (濡れ手で泡). This is a common saying meaning to be able to do something well without any great effort.

Strategy 10: Conceal a Sword behind a Smile

1. These various *Lu*'s are all written with different Chinese characters. There is no relationship between either of the men or between the men and the city.

Strategy 13: Beat the Grass, Surprise the Snake

1. *Return*, the twenty-fourth hexagram, *Fu*, of the *I Ching*. Although there is no direct quote here, the inclusion of the hexagram's title would seem to require some note. Relevant sections might be as follows. In the Commentary it states:

> With *Return*, "understanding" means that the hard (yang) comes back. Moving, by means of order, things are put into action. With this, going out and coming back in are performed faultlessly, and friends arrive without blame.

In the first of the six lines, which represent the nuances of the hexagrams, we find the following: "Return without going too far. This will not bring regret. Fundamental good fortune." And in the sixth line, this cautionary note appears: "To return in confusion is ill-omened. There will be calamity and poor vision. If the army is moved in this way, there will be great failure in the end."

Strategy 14: Borrow the Corpse, Revive Its Soul

1. From the fourth hexagram, *Meng*, from the *I Ching*. In the Commentary it states: "*You do not seek after a foolish youth; a foolish youth will seek after you*, and respond to your will."

   Further, in the first line, we find this comment: "Develop the foolish youth. It is beneficial to make an example of someone. If you loosen his shackles and go forward, there will be regret;" in the second line, "Embrace the foolish youth. Good fortune." And a cautionary note in the third line concerning the character of the foolish youth you may be using: "Do not take this woman to wife. If she sees a young man with money, she will not act properly, and there will be no benefit."

Strategy 15: Pacify the Tiger Then Lead It from the Mountain

1. From the thirty-ninth hexagram, *Chien*, of the *I Ching*. It is taken directly from the third line: "If you go, there will be obstruction; if he comes, the opposite." In the Commentary, it states that "*obstruction* means difficulty. It is steep going ahead. Recognize the danger, and be able to stop. This is wisdom."

2. Because of Han Hsin's stand against the Chao, "To encamp with one's back to a river" is now translated in dictionaries as "to make a last stand."

Strategy 16: If You Covet It, Leave It Alone

1. From the fifth hexagram, *Hsu*, of the *I Ching*. In the Commentary, it states:

   Waiting means to be patient. There is steep going in front of you. Be firm (yang) and strong, do not fall down the slope; thus you will not be in distress. If *in waiting there is sincerity, light*, and truth, there will be good fortune; you will be in the position given to you by Heaven, thus correct and hitting the target. "There is benefit in crossing a great river" means that there is merit in moving on.

2. *T'sai ken tan* (*Vegetable Root Discourses*). Late Ming-period book written by the hermit-scholar Hung Ying-ming. Its 357 verses in prose-poetry express the meanings of Taoism, Confucianism, Zen, and Buddhism in general. It advocates living with truly humanistic values rather than adhering to formal ideals that overlook the foibles and weakness of mankind. The author believes in living with our fellow human beings' mistakes.

Strategy 17: Cast a Brick, Pull in Jade

1. From the fourth hexagram. In the sixth line, it states the following: "Strike the foolish youth. But there is no benefit in making him an enemy. It is beneficial to prevent future harm." The Commentary on that line says that "the benefit of preventing future harm is that upper and lower will be in (proper) order."

2. Hsiung-nu. A Turkish-speaking people living in Mongolia. The northern group of this tribe went westward, where they became known as the Huns.

3. *Huai Nan Tzu*. A second-century B.C. book of twenty-one chapters containing the Taoist and syncretic writings of Liu An, prince of Huai Nan (d. 122 B.C.). Liu An was the grandson of Kao Tsu, the founder of the Han dynasty, and surrounded himself with scholars at his court. Privilege and philosophy were

perhaps not enough for him, as he plotted a rebellion and, upon its failure, was forced to commit suicide.

4. *Hsun Tzu*. A book by the third-century B.C. philosopher of the same name. Partly Taoist, partly authoritarian, it is said to have greatly influenced the dictatorial policies of the First Emperor. Hsun Tzu believed strongly in logic, order, proper economy, and progress. The above-mentioned Han Fei Tzu was one of his pupils.

Strategy 18: To Catch a Thief, Catch His King

1. From the second hexagram, *Kun*, of the *I Ching*.

2. This is because a dragon is at home fighting in either the water or the air.

Strategy 19: Pull the Firewood from under the Kettle

1. Noting the two trigrams, Heaven and Lake, that make up the tenth hexagram, *Lu*, of the *I Ching*. In the Judgment, it makes the following statement: "Stepping on the tiger's tail. It does not bite. Penetrating understanding." In the first line, we find this: "Walking on without artifice. He advances without blame." The Commentary on the third line is cautionary: "The one-eyed man is able to see, but with insufficient clarity. The lame man is able to walk on, but cannot keep up with others. (Stepping on the tiger's tail and) being bitten is an ill omen, as they are in an inappropriate situation. The warrior (inferior) acts for the great prince (superior), and his will is firm." The fourth line adds this note: "Stepping on the tiger's tail with great apprehension ends with good fortune."

2. This was a sort of Confucian harangue on filial piety, i.e., the commander's relationship to the troops being one of parent to child, which the soldiers would have presumably understood and taken to heart; or possibly because they were needlessly endangering themselves.

Strategy 20: Disturb the Water, Grab the Fish

1. From the seventeenth hexagram, *Sui*, of the *I Ching*. In the Image, it states: "Thunder in the middle of the Lake means *Following. The Gentleman faces the evening and rests with ease.*"

In the Commentary, it states: "*Following* the hard (yang) comes and goes under the soft (yin). *Following* moves with pleasure. There is great penetration and truth, and no blame. All under Heaven follow the moment. The timing of *Following* is significant, indeed."

Strategy 21: The Golden Cicada Sheds Its Shell

1. From the eighteenth hexagram, *Ku*, of the *I Ching*. In the Commentary, it states:

> *From Stagnation Comes the New* is the hard (yang) above and the soft (yin) below. *It follows that stopping means, "From stagnation comes the new." From Stagnation Comes the New* penetrates everywhere and administers all under Heaven. "It is beneficial to cross a great river" means that one can go forth with things to do. Before mobilization, three days; after mobilization, three days. If there is an end, there will have been a beginning: This is the way Heaven proceeds.

Strategy 22: Bar the Door, Grab the Thief

1. From the twenty-third hexagram, *Po*, of the *I Ching*. In the Judgment, it states: "*Splitting Apart; there is no advantage in giving chase.*"

In the Commentary, it states:

> *Splitting Apart* is tearing away. The soft (yin) changes the hard (yang). That there is no benefit in having some place to go means that men of little character may become influential. Follow order and come to a stop. Contemplate the image (a Mountain [crumbling?] over the Earth). The Gentleman respects the cycle of decrease and increase, of waxing and waning, for this is the way Heaven proceeds.

2. *Wu Tzu*. A Chinese classic on warfare in six strategies, written by Wu Ch'i (d. 381 B.C.). Quoted extensively in the Lionel Giles translation of Sun Tzu's *The Art of War*.

Strategy 23: Befriend Those at a Distance, Attack Those Nearby

1. From the thirty-eighth hexagram, *K'uei*, of the *I Ching*. In the Commentary, it states: "Heaven and Earth *conflict*, but their achievements are the same; men and women *conflict*, but their emotions are mutually understood. The Ten Thousand Things *conflict*, but their affairs are all akin." In the Image, it tells us that "*Fire above, the Lake below*. By this, the Gentleman knows their similarities and differences."

Strategy 24: Borrow a Road, Attack Kuo

1. From the forty-seventh hexagram, *K'un*, of the *I Ching*. In the Judgment, it states: "*Dilemma*. Penetrating understanding. Correctness; the mature man has good fortune without blame. *When there are words, they will not be believed.*" In the Commentary, it states:

    Dilemma; the hard (yang) is covered over. With a steep road, be joyful. Only the Gentleman does not lose his penetrating understanding when in a painful situation. "Correctness; the mature man has good fortune" means that he is firm and hitting the target. *"When there are words, they will not be believed"* means that too much respect for what is spoken brings distress.

Strategy 25: Steal the Beams, Replace the Pillars

1. From the sixty-fourth hexagram, *Wei Chi*, of the *I Ching*. In the Image, it states: "Fire over Water means *Not Yet Finished*. The Gentleman is circumspect, differentiates things, and keeps them in their [proper] places." In the second line, it states: "Brake the wheels. Correctness will bring good fortune."

Strategy 26: Point to the Mulberry, Berate the Pagoda Tree

1. From the seventh hexagram, *Shih*, of the *I Ching*. In the Commentary, it states:

    A *Throng* is a mass of people. Correctness is in being straightforward. If you are straightforward in leading the people well, you can become a ruler. Firm and unwavering, you obtain a response; *act with severity, and there will be order*. Thus, though the world be in pain, the people will follow you. Good fortune. How could there be blame?

2. *Seven Books on the Martial Arts* (or *Martial Strategies*). These are difficult to identify, but in the bibliography to Giles's translation of *The Art of War*, he lists eight of the "old Chinese treatises of war," the first six of which, plus *The Art of War*, "were prescribed for military training" during the Sung dynasty. They are the following, but the dates noted are questionable:

    1. *Wu Tzu*, by Wu Ch'i (d. 381 B.C.).
    2. *Ssu-ma Fa*, possibly by Sze Ma Jang-chu of the sixth century B.C.
    3. *Liu T'ao*, by Lu Wang of the twelfth century B.C.
    4. *Wei Liao Tzu*, by Wei Liao of the fourth century B.C.
    5. *San Lueh*, by Huang-shih Kung of the second century B.C.
    6. *Li Wei Kung Wen Tui*, author and date unknown.

Strategy 27: Feign Stupidity, Do Not Be Injudicious

1. From the third hexagram, *Chun*, of the *I Ching*. In the Image, it states: "*Clouds and thunder indicate Birth. Thus, the Gentleman* brings order to the land, and sets things aright." And in the Commentary, it states: "*Birth*; in the beginning, hard (yang) and soft (yin) mix together, and parturition is difficult: movement in the midst of danger. Great penetrating wisdom and correctness; the movement of thunder and rain brings fulfillment." "Birth" can also be understood as "difficulty in the beginning."

Strategy 28: Send Them to the Roof, Remove the Ladder

1. From the twenty-first hexagram, *Shih Ho*, of the *I Ching*. In the third line, it states: "Chewing dried meat, he encounters poison; slight regret, but no blame." In the Commentary on the third line, we find: "Encountering poison; his position crumbles."

2. The capital of the state of Manipur in northeast India. It was here that the Japanese army's plan for the invasion of India was thwarted by a disastrous defeat in July 1944. The defeat was brought about partly by Lieutenant General Mutaguchi's ill-advised strategy for the logistics of transporting rations.

3. Take action only after looking into the fine details. Exercise extreme caution. Sometimes used sarcastically as criticism of cowardice.

Strategy 29: Make the Flowers Bloom on the Tree

1. From the fifty-third hexagram, *Chien*, of the *I Ching*. In the ninth line, it states: "The wild goose gradually progresses over the broad highway. Its feathers can be used for ceremonies. Well-omened." In the Commentary on the ninth line, it states: "Its feathers may be used for ceremonies. Well-omened, but this cannot be in a chaotic way."

Strategy 30: Quit as Guest, Take Over as Host

1. From the fifty-third hexagram of the *I Ching*. In the Commentary, it states:

   Advance is in gradual progress. A woman given in marriage is well-omened. She advances in position, and there is merit in going forward. Advancing with correctness, you can make your own territory correct. Your position is firm (yang), and you gain the center. Pause and be docile; move without going to extremes.

Strategy 31: Strategy of the Beautiful Woman

1. From the fifty-third hexagram of the *I Ching*. In the Commentary on the third line, it states: "The husband goes out to the front, but does not return; he separates from his compatriots. His wife conceives, but does not deliver: she has lost her way. *It is beneficial to suppress the enemy; this is pliability and concomitant protection.*"

2. These "Chous" are homonyms; the Chinese characters and meanings are different.

Strategy 33: Create a Rift

1. From the eighth hexagram, *Pi*, in the *I Ching*. In the Commentary on the second line, it states: *"If you can stay on familiar terms with those among your own, you will not lose yourself."*

   In the Commentary, it states:

   > Familiarity is well-omened. Familiarity will help. The lower follows proper order. Looking for omens, if you are fundamentally and consistently correct, there will be no blame. For this reason, you will be strong and will hit the target. Those still uneasy will approach, and upper and lower will respond mutually. The latecomer is ill-omened; his way will be cut off.

Strategy 34: The Strategy of Self-Injury

1. From the fifth hexagram. Verbatim in the Commentary on the fifth line.

2. While this strategy was perhaps not used, the battle itself has long grasped the imagination of the Chinese, and it has been celebrated in poetry and travel diaries for centuries.

Strategy 35: The Strategy of Links

1. From the seventh hexagram, *Shih*, of the *I Ching*. In the second line, it states: "The commander is there and unwobbling; good fortune. He receives Heaven's favor. Three times the ruler bestows his orders. He cares for his entire vast territory."

   The term *Shih* (師) is explained in a number of ways by scholars of the *I Ching*. It means variously master, teacher, army, battle, or throng; but with the *I Ching*, it has often been interpreted as "army" and "throng." The fact is that the Chinese characters that entitle the hexagrams are rather fluid in meaning, and probably intentionally so. In Strategies 26, 35, and 36, they are defined according to context.

2. Golden Horde. The Khanate of Kipchak, initially ruled by Batu (1227–55), a grandson of Genghis Khan. It was centered in the area of the lower Volga River and more or less dominated South Russia until the fifteenth century.

Strategy 36: Retreat Is Considered the Best

1. From the seventh hexagram, *Shih*, of the *I Ching*. In the Commentary on the fourth line, it states: "There is no blame in retreating and taking shelter; doing so one will not yet have lost his ordinary condition."

2. The shattered jewel. The traditional image in Japan of an honorable or glorious death uses the metaphor of shattering a jewel. This was an ideal of the samurai, and most recently of the kamikaze and even the common soldiers in the army. A Japanese proverb has it that "It is better to be shattered like a jewel than to be whole like a clay tile."

3. "Chickens' ribs" (鶏肋) is a common expression in China and Japan for something that, in the end, is not worth fussing over: something of little value that one nonetheless hesitates to throw away.

4. Kunisada Chuji (1810–50). A famous Edo-period gambler and criminal. Obese, pasty, and given to extravagant language, he was a cruel murderer and fugitive. He finally collapsed from apoplexy, was captured, sent to Edo, and executed. He thereafter became a popular subject for the Kabuki theater and professional storytellers.

BIBLIOGRAPHY

WORKS IN ORIENTAL LANGUAGES

Ekkyo. Vols. 1 & 2. Translated by Takada Shinji and Goto Motomi. Tokyo: Iwanami Bunsho, 2004.

Koyogunkan, Gorinnosho, Hagakure. Translated and edited by Sagara Toru. Tokyo: Chikuma Shobo, 1964.

Moriya, Hiroshi. *Heiho Sanjurokkei.* Tokyo: Chiteki Shuppansha, 1993.

Moriya, Hiroshi. *Heiho Sanjurokkei.* Tokyo: Mikasa Shobo, no date given.

Sonshi-Goshi. Edited by Miura Yoshiaki. Tokyo: Meiji Shoin, 2002.

WORKS IN ENGLISH

Basic Writings of Mo Tzu, Hsun Tzu, and Han Fei Tzu. Translated by Burton Watson. New York: Columbia University Press, 1967.

Ch'ien Ssu-ma. *Records of the Historian.* Translated by Burton Watson. New York: Columbia University Press, 1958.

Fairbank, John K., Edwin O. Reischauer, and Albert M. Craig. *East Asia: Tradition and Transformation.* Boston: Houghton Mifflin Co., 1973.

Giles, Herbert A. *History of Chinese Literature.* New York: D. Appleton and Company, 1923.

Hung, Ying-ming. *Roots of Wisdom: Saikontan.* Translated by William Scott Wilson. Tokyo: Kodansha International, 1985.

WORKS IN CHINESE AND ENGLISH

Sun Tzu on the Art of War. Translated and annotated by Lionel Giles. Shanghai: 1910.

（英文版）兵法三十六計
The 36 Secret Strategies of the Martial Arts

2008年1月25日　第1刷発行

著　者　　守屋　洋
英　訳　　ウィリアム・スコット・ウィルソン
発行者　　富田　充
発行所　　講談社インターナショナル株式会社
　　　　　〒112-8652 東京都文京区音羽1-17-14
　　　　　電話　03-3944-6493（編集部）
　　　　　　　　03-3944-6492（営業部・業務部）
　　　　　ホームページ　www.kodansha-intl.com
印刷・製本所　　大日本印刷株式会社